Praise for The Nonfiction

MW00529341

"As someone who has been writing and pr⟨⟩ decades, I can tell you that Stephanie Cha⟨⟩ ing. *The Nonfiction Book Marketing Plan* is an essential guide to getting more exposure for you and your books online. This book should be on every author's bookshelf!"

— **Dan Poynter**, Author of *The Self-Publishing Manual: How to Write, Print and Sell Your Own Book*, www.ParaPublishing.com

"Nobody knows internet marketing for authors like Stephanie Chandler! This book is loaded with strategies that will help you sell more books online."

–**Brian Jud**, Executive Director of SPAN and author of *How to Make Real Money Selling Books*

"Stephanie has been around the 'book block' many times in her jam-packed career—one full of big-time risk and reward. She holds nothing back here, sharing the vast wealth of her experience in the nonfiction realm. If publishing nonfiction is your game, this book provides an invaluable success blueprint, from someone who's done so many things right for a long time. Buy it."

— **Peter Bowerman**, Author *The Well-Fed Writer* and *The Well-Fed Self-Publisher*

"Stephanie Chandler's *The Nonfiction Book Marketing Plan* is chock-full of proven ideas for marketing your books, your program, and yourself. If you're a nonfiction author who really wants to sell books, this is an invaluable resource. Highly recommended."

— **Joel Friedlander**, www.TheBookDesigner.com

"Essential reading for anyone who wants to be a successful writer in the digital age. This is a tremendous guide that will enable you to take advantage of the amazing opportunities for sharing your passion for your work."

— **Michael Larsen**, Author of *How to Write a Book Proposal*, co-director of the San Francisco Writers Conference

"At last, a book for nonfiction authors written by a savvy business consultant that integrates the dos and don'ts of writing and publishing with credible tips for leveraging your book into opportunities and profits. Filled with concise ideas, tips, examples, personal experiences, and author profiles."

— **Roger C. Parker**, www.PublishedandProfitable.com

"Stephanie Chandler's new release, *The Nonfiction Book Marketing Plan*, is a bible for the nonfiction author . . . a thorough, logical, step-by-step guide that is priceless in navigating this explosive world of options when it comes to publishing, promotion, and marketing a book. Finally, nonfiction authors have directions of their own, and don't have to hunt amongst all the fiction advice to find guidance that fits their needs. A professional guidebook to walk you through the all-too-many issues involved in getting your book into the hands of readers."

— **C. Hope Clark**, Editor www.FundsforWriters.com, Author of *The Shy Writer Reborn*

"If you're looking for a checklist to design and carry out a book marketing plan, here it is. Stephanie has provided a great overview for generating book sales."

— **John Kremer**, Author of *1001 Ways to Market Your Books*

THE
NONFICTION
BOOK

MARKETING PLAN:

*Online and Offline
Promotion Strategies
to Build Your Audience
and Sell More Books*

STEPHANIE CHANDLER

*Write on!
Stephanie
Chandler*

Published by

AUTHORITY
PUBLISHING

The Nonfiction Book Marketing Plan: Online and Offline Promotion Strategies to Build Your Audience and Sell More Books
By Stephanie Chandler

1. Business & Economics: E-Commerce – Internet Marketing 2. Business & Economics: Marketing – General 3. Business & Economics: Advertising & Promotion

ISBN: 978-1-935953-54-8

Cover design by Lewis Agrell

Book design by Sue Balcer

The text of this book is set in Adobe Garamond Pro

Printed in the United States of America

AUTHORITY
PUBLISHING

Authority Publishing
11230 Gold Express Dr. #310-413
Gold River, CA 95670
800-877-1097
www.AuthorityPublishing.com

Dedication

This book is dedicated to the brilliant members of my mastermind group: Karl Palachuk, Jenifer Novak Landers, Patrick Schwerdtfeger, John Armato, Adam Frick, Jason Davis, Jake Romero, Sharon Broughton, and Julie Yarbrough. Everyone should be lucky enough to be part of a mastermind group! It's my favorite event that I attend each month, and I am eternally grateful for the support, encouragement, friendship, and ideas spawned from this group of immensely talented business owners.

Table of Contents

Part 2: Book Launch

Part 3: After the Book is Released

Chapter 7: Offline Marketing Tactics 135

Chapter 8: Online Marketing Tactics

Introduction

I SET OUT IN THIS WORLD to be a novelist. I have loved writing for as long as I can remember, and when you love to write you often come to believe that you should write the Great American Novel. Unfortunately, I quickly learned that I wasn't destined to write fiction. I lacked the imagination needed to invent stories, and my initial efforts were downright awful.

Along the way I accidentally discovered that I had a passion for writing nonfiction, which can combine the joys of teaching (something I have also long had a passion for) with the creativity of writing; it involves storytelling based on facts, which for me are a lot easier to produce than figments of my imagination.

I am sharing this with you because my hope is that, as a nonfiction writer, you will develop the same pride and joy that fiction writers experience. I have met so many nonfiction writers over the years who don't really "own" their author status or believe that the books they produce have artistic value. Writing nonfiction is a craft that is just as important and creative and powerful as writing fiction. It took me a long time to realize and embrace this reality. Not everyone can produce great fiction, but not everyone can produce great nonfiction, either. You have a skill that few others possess.

Writing a book is something that a reported 80% of people would like to do, but only a small percentage will actually follow that dream through to completion. If you're reading this book, you're on that journey. You may not be done with your first manuscript yet, or you may have many books to your credit already. Wherever you are in the writing journey, you are making it happen. You are achieving a dream that exists on so many people's bucket lists—and that is something to be proud of.

After you celebrate the monumental achievement of writing and publishing a book, you are then faced with the hardest task of all: marketing. My goal in writing this book is to make the challenge ahead of you a little bit easier. Included throughout *The Nonfiction Book Marketing Plan* are tried and true methods for promoting your work. You probably won't use them all, but you can find and implement the tactics that fit your needs and goals.

At the end of each chapter, I have included an interview with a nonfiction author so that you can also learn from their experiences. No two authors have exactly the same journey, and there is power in learning from each other.

My Author Journey

If you've read any of my previous books or you've seen me speak at an event, you probably already know about my history. I won't be offended if you skip ahead to chapter one! For everyone else, following is an overview about how I ended up writing nonfiction, and discovering the path I was supposed to travel, even though it was never really in my plans.

In 2003, I quit my Silicon Valley sales job and opened a 2,800 square-foot new and used bookstore in Sacramento, California. Nearly everyone I knew thought I had lost my mind. I don't blame them. I swapped a $4 million annual sales quota to sell $4 paperbacks, which doesn't sound like the smartest decision I've ever heard.

I was burnt out on corporate America and ready for a big lifestyle change. As a long-time book lover, I fell for the romantic notion of running a bookstore, and my big master plan was that I would sit in the back office and write novels. And so the store was built from the ground up, shelf by shelf, with 20,000 books put into inventory. I also adopted two fat adult cats from the SPCA, because any bookstore worth visiting should have a store cat.

About six weeks after the store opened, I remember standing at the checkout counter, looking around the store and thinking to myself, "Holy crap. What have I done?" I didn't want to run a retail store. There were a million headaches I hadn't anticipated. After years in software sales, running around from place to place meeting with clients each day, I was suddenly trapped in a building from 9 a.m. to 6 p.m. six days per week. I didn't enjoy managing minimum wage employees. There were cockroaches visiting from the restaurant next door. There were visits from the occasional homeless person and numerous customers who were weird, unstable, and even threatening. We were also robbed one day, while my toughest-looking, tattooed employee was running the register.

To make matters worse, I had opened the store in a strip mall that didn't have a lot of street visibility. I spent thousands of dollars on expensive phone book ads, coupon mailers, and other advertising methods that weren't working at the level I had hoped. I realized I had no choice but to find other marketing methods that produced better results.

I started by learning about search engine optimization (SEO), and was amazed at how easy it was to get the store website to the top of Google search results—and that effort brought in far more shoppers. Then we started selling online and promoting store events online. I reached out to local media and was able to get some big coverage for the store. All of these efforts began to add up, and before I knew it, the store was profitable and I could afford to have a staff keep it running.

While all of this was going on, I decided to start a writer's group at the store and explore my dream of writing a novel. I began by sharing short stories with the group, and while nobody ever said the words, I could tell my stories weren't very good. It was a sad day when I realized that I wasn't meant to write fiction.

Soon my Silicon Valley friends started making the two-hour drive up to Sacramento to see my store in action. Many said that they wanted some of that entrepreneurial spirit to rub off on them. They were frustrated with their jobs, but afraid to take a big leap of faith and do what I did. I will forever be grateful for those visits, emails, and phone calls because it sparked something in me that I wasn't expecting. It occurred to me that perhaps I could help them realize that there could be life after corporate America.

I had read dozens of business books during the year I spent planning my corporate exodus, yet they were all pretty much the same. None of them addressed some of the real-world issues I faced, like how to negotiate a commercial lease (I scored three months of free rent for my store!), how to create an operations manual, and what was involved in managing employees. I realized that I could follow Toni Morrison's advice: "If there is a book you want to read, but it hasn't been written yet, then you must write it."

And so I began writing my first book, which became *The Business Startup Checklist and Planning Guide: Seize Your Entrepreneurial Dreams!* That year I attended the San Francisco Writer's Conference, an experience that was a major turning point in my career. I had the opportunity to participate in "speed dating with agents," where I sat in front of literary agents for two minutes each and pitched my book. Many requested book proposals, so I returned home and sent them out, eagerly awaiting an offer for a book deal.

But then the rejections followed, most telling me that I didn't have a platform. I was unclear about what that meant until I received a call on my cell phone one day while I was at the bookstore. It was Michael Larsen, a well-known and respected literary agent in San Francisco. He told me that he liked my work, but that nobody knew who I was. I needed to go out and build a platform, which meant that I should be speaking to thousands of people each year. When I suggested that was like putting the cart before the horse and that I'd get invited to speak once I had a book available, he agreed but said that big publishing houses wanted authors to come to them with a built-in audience. They weren't in the business of taking risks, so once I had an audience I would be more likely to land a book deal.

I will forever be grateful to Mike Larsen for taking the time to call me that day. He shaped my future in more ways than he will ever know, and he remains a dear friend.

After that call, I had to figure out what to do. I didn't want to become a road warrior, but I needed to find an audience. Then I realized that I'd had some good success with marketing the bookstore online. Perhaps I could find my audience of readers with a website.

I really had no idea what I was doing, but I decided I'd figure it out as I went along. I quickly launched a website, http://BusinessInfoGuide.com, with the goal of attracting aspiring entrepreneurs. I started writing articles and sharing resources, and the more I wrote, the more traffic the site received. I added a sign-up box for an e-newsletter, and sent the first edition out to a grand total of eight subscribers.

Since I was impatient with the prospect of waiting for a traditional book deal, I decided to self-publish. I hired a custom publishing company to help with the production since I didn't have the time or inclination to deal with finding contractors, getting bids for printers, and setting up distribution.

I decided to list the book for pre-sale two months before it was in print, and that darn book started selling immediately. That was when I truly began to understand the power of marketing online. I also understood where the big publishers were coming from. If I hadn't built an audience, my book wouldn't be selling. I had to go find my readers.

After that, I decided I wanted to sell information products on the site in the form of workbooks and special reports. I looked for a book on how to do so, but couldn't find one so I studied how other people were selling their products and tried to model their strategies. I listed two products for sale and they began selling immediately. It was truly astounding.

Since nobody had written a book about how to create and sell information products, I set out to write book number two. But by then I had significant website traffic and a growing email list, which meant I had an audience. I wrote a book proposal and sent it to exactly two publishers. About a month later I signed a deal with John Wiley and Sons to publish *From Entrepreneur to Infopreneur: Make Money with Books, eBooks, and Information Products*.

That book was a game-changer for me because it helped me reach a whole new audience. The book sold well and attracted a bigger following. Before I knew it, I was receiving invitations to speak at events, as well as inquiries about consulting. I suddenly found myself with a whole new career I hadn't planned on.

Thankfully the bookstore was pretty much running itself by then. I showed up once or twice a week to deal with cash and paychecks, but spent most of my time at my home office, writing, consulting and traveling to speaking engagements.

After that, I scheduled lunch with a literary agent I'd met at the San Francisco Writer's Conference two years earlier. She wanted to hear about the business book idea I was working on. I brought along a copy of a workbook I was selling from my site called *Online Marketing for Authors*. I thought some of her clients might be interested in a copy. She thumbed through it while I rambled on about my business book idea, and then she interrupted me and said, "I think I can sell this. Are you interested in selling it?" It hadn't even occurred to me, but I agreed. Several weeks later, she brought me a deal from Quill Driver Books, and they renamed the book: *The Author's Guide to Building an Online Platform: Leveraging the Internet to Sell More Books*. (I still think my previous title was better, but when you sell the rights to your book, you give up all control.)

After that, my agent sold my next book to Career Press: *LEAP! 101 Ways to Grow Your Business*. In the midst of all of this, I had increasing resentment for the bookstore. It felt like a weight on my shoulders that I needed to release. Fortunately, it was profitable enough to put up for sale, and I ended up finding a buyer and closing the transaction on May 31, 2007—my son's first birthday.

With so much free time to focus on my consulting business and writing, I began to realize that I wasn't too happy with my traditional book deals. I was earning around $1 per book sold, which meant that the twice-yearly royalty checks were disappointing. Ebook sales were also becoming more popular, yet I earned even less for those and didn't have the right to sell my own ebooks through my website.

A lot of my consulting clients were also asking me for guidance on how to get their books published, and many were choosing the self-publishing route. Eventually I realized that I could help them, and I launched Authority Publishing in 2008. I decided to focus on publishing nonfiction books, with the goal of providing high-quality publishing production services and personalized customer service. The "big box" self-publishing firms were treating authors like commodities. They were staffed by young college students and people who had no experience in publishing, operating giant call centers and producing books with templates for covers and interiors. They would also publish anything in exchange for a check. I knew I could do better.

This decision also forced me to hire a team of people to help. I wasn't an editor or a book designer, so I set out to find talented, experienced people to manage these tasks. One big benefit was that I began to shift my business model. My income was no longer dependent on selling my time by consulting alone. I was now generating income by outsourcing most tasks to other people, which freed me up to do more of the things I most enjoyed (like writing!).

Of course it only made sense that I would return to self-publishing and produce my subsequent books under my own imprint. I was grateful for the control that I had regained in doing this. With my previous books, I had covers designed that I didn't like, but it didn't matter. The publisher chose the cover whether I liked it or not. For one of my books, I was told to remove an entire chapter so that I would stay within the designated page count (and reduce printing costs). This was incredibly frustrating for me, though I turned lemons into lemonade and instead made the chapter available to readers as a bonus download from my website, which helped to drive traffic from readers back to my site.

My subsequent books published through Authority Publishing have included:

- *Booked Up! How to Write, Publish, and Promote a Book to Grow Your Business*

- *The Conference Catcher: An Organized Journal for Capturing Ideas, Resources, and Action Items at Educational Conferences, Trade Shows, and Events*

- *Own Your Niche: Hype-Free Internet Marketing Tactics to Establish Authority in Your Field and Promote Your Service-Based Business.*

I also converted a former information product, a workbook I sold through my site, into a book: *How to Start and Run a Used Bookstore: A Bookstore Owner's Essential Toolkit with Real-World Insights, Strategies, Forms, and Procedures.*

In recent years, I have continued to develop my publishing business and cultivate the two target audiences I most want to reach: nonfiction authors and service-based business owners. We added social media marketing services to the menu of options at Authority Publishing. In 2010, I launched the Nonfiction Writers Conference, a virtual event that includes 15 speakers over three days. As I finish writing this book (I always write the introduction last!), I am in the process of launching the Nonfiction Authors Association, an online site where I hope to build a community of authors and continue with ongoing marketing education for members.

As I write this, I am in my tenth year of entrepreneurship, my eighth year as a published author, and this is my ninth book! It has been an incredible journey, and one that I never could have imagined for myself. I often say that my path found me. If I still had that bookstore, and was struggling to write novels, I'd probably be miserable and broke! Fortunately, I followed my gut and took some turns along the path that I wasn't expecting, which has led me to meet some wonderful people and build a career that I am grateful for every day.

And so this book is born from these experiences. I hope that you will discover ideas and opportunities that help you carve out your own path, which may look very different from mine. That's the greatest part of being a writer and an entrepreneur. No two journeys are the same. But we can still learn from each other. I hope you'll visit me through any of my websites and let me know how these strategies have worked for you.

- **http://NonfictionAuthorsAssociation.com** – Association for Nonfiction Authors, providing a supportive community for members to connect, learn, and support each other.

- **http://NonfictionWritersConference.com** – The only online conference of its kind for nonfiction authors. Conducted annually with 15 speakers over three days.

- **http://AuthorityPublishing.com** – Specializing in custom publishing for nonfiction books and social media marketing services for authors.

- **http://BusinessInfoGuide.com** – Resources for entrepreneurs. Guest articles and interviews welcome. Look for the "contribute" link on the main navigation menu.

- **http://StephanieChandler.com** – Official author/speaker website.

PART ONE:

Before the Book is Published (Ideally)

Chapter 1:
Build the Foundation

"If you don't have time to read, you don't have
the time (or the tools) to write. Simple as that."
— Stephen King

IN AN IDEAL WORLD, you are reading *The Nonfiction Book Marketing Plan* book before you've published your book because that will give you time to begin building your audience before your book is launched. But I realize that's not likely for most who read this book. The good news is that you can start marketing at any time because nonfiction books usually don't have an expiration date. The point is to just get started, no matter where you are in the publishing and promotion process, and commit to seeing it through.

Commitment is hugely important for authors. I see authors struggle with this all of the time. They get excited to release the book, and then realize it takes work to deal with marketing. Soon, other priorities take over and the book stops selling, and then the author gets frustrated. I call this "author post-partum," and the only cure is to re-engage and celebrate the small wins because eventually those add up.

The reality is that your book is going to compete with millions of titles. Just because it's available on Amazon.com doesn't mean that it will sell or that readers will find it. *You've got to build an audience and lead them to your book.* This takes a serious level of commitment and ongoing effort.

You might worry because you have a day job and don't have time for marketing. Well, welcome to the club! Most *New York Times* bestselling authors have day jobs. You managed to find time to write your book, and now you must find time to do the work to help it sell.

Many authors have told me that they hate marketing. I get it. I like to compare it to gardening. Some people love gardening, but I'm not one of them. I don't like dirt or bugs or the grunt work involved in cultivating a beautiful yard. But what I do enjoy is the end result. I want a beautiful yard, and so I begrudgingly do the work in order to reap the long-term rewards.

Imagine what would happen if you planted just three seeds in your yard every day. Over time you'd have a lush, beautiful garden! Marketing works the same way. A little effort every day adds up to big rewards, but you've got to do the work. If you ignore your yard, it will grow weeds while your plants die. I'm quite sure you don't want that same fate for your book, otherwise you wouldn't be reading this book!

You can also find ways to enjoy the work. When I work in my yard, I crank up music and try to make it fun. I take breaks to play with my dog and my kid. I make the best of it. I also hired a landscaper to come in weekly and handle the maintenance. You can certainly outsource some of the marketing tasks that you don't like! And when you do the work, you might even find that there are some tasks you actually enjoy.

I also know that when we resist something, it can seem harder than it really is. For example, if you loathe having to do your dishes every day, it's going to make that job even more painful. You will be filled with dread before you even start! It will undoubtedly affect your mood and make it feel like a much bigger deal than it actually is. But if you stopped resisting it—if you made the decision to stop dreading the chore and instead focused on getting it done, then appreciated the beauty of a clean kitchen, that chore wouldn't seem nearly as painful! Can you at least try that with marketing?

I will step down off my soapbox now and let you embark on this journey. My goal here is to provide you with many do-it-yourself tactics to help you plant your marketing garden. Many of these tasks can also be outsourced, if that is what you choose. And what I know for sure is that when you see these things through, you will find many, many rewards from your efforts. There is nothing better than the feeling of hearing from a reader who has been affected by your work. I keep all of those messages in files that I can refer to later, when I'm having a rough day or just need a boost. Yes, it's hard work. But I wouldn't trade the journey for anything, and my hope is that you will feel the same way.

Define Your Goals

Before you begin to think about marketing plans for your book, you need to first be clear about your goals. For some authors, the only thing that matters is book sales, and that is just fine, though the reality is that it's not easy to make a living with a book. If you're lucky, you will probably earn between $5 to $15 per book, depending on the sales channel—and that's if you self-publish. Traditionally published authors typically earn around $1 per book sold through a retail outlet! Regardless of how much you earn for each book, you would probably have to sell a truckload of books each month to earn a living.

For the majority of nonfiction authors, books are a sideline. You probably have a day job, a family, and a life. Sales earned from your book can be a nice supplement to that. But if you want to make real money with your book, then also consider different ways you can leverage your book for other opportunities.

A book is your ticket to open doors, and there are many ways you can use your book to reach personal goals and to generate bigger revenues, especially if you are already a business owner (or you want to be). Here are some options:

- Attract new clients by giving copies of your book to prospects.
- Reach high-profile contacts by sending them a copy.
- Get booked for speaking engagements.
- Attract media interviews and leverage those to promote your business.
- Sell books in bulk to companies, trade associations, chain stores, and schools.
- Build new revenue streams around your book, such as companion coaching programs, events, or information products.
- Capture corporate sponsorship dollars.
- Build a following to attract readers for future books.
- Get paid to write for magazines and websites.

For me personally, I'm never very interested in my total book sales numbers because I'm far more focused on how my books help me serve my target audience, build a reputation and grow my business. Each book I've written has brought substantial opportunities including new clients, corporate spon-sorships, spokesperson roles, paid blogging opportunities, a column that I write for the *Forbes* blog, speaking engagements, partnerships with peers, bulk sales, and much more. So my goals center around how each book will benefit my business and lead to more of the opportunities I want to create.

Chapter 10 discusses revenue generating strategies, so we'll go into great depth there. However, it's important to be clear about your goals before you build your marketing plan because your goals will affect your marketing decisions.

Answer these questions for yourself:

1. What do I ultimately want to accomplish?

2. What opportunities can I create with my book?

3. How can I stretch out of my comfort zone?

4. What do I need to learn to be successful?

5. Who are some people I can model on my way to achieving my goals?

6. How much time can I commit each week to pursuing my goals?

7. What would my life look like if I reached these goals?

Identify Your Target Audience

Narrowing your focus to an ideal target audience can have a tremendous impact on the results you see from your book marketing efforts. When you are clear about *who* it is you want to reach, it makes it easier for your audience to connect with you and your book.

Ideally, you gave this some thought before you wrote your book, but even if you didn't, it's not too late! Establishing a niche focus will help you better connect with the needs of your ideal readers (target audience). And when you cast the net too wide, you actually risk missing out on book sales because you lack focus.

For example, imagine you are venturing into your first sales job at a software company and need to learn about sales immediately. While perus-ing sales books you find dozens that cover general sales strategies, but then you discover one called, "Software Sales Success: How to Become the Top

Sales Person in Your Technology Company." Which book are you most likely to buy? (I wish there had been a book like this when I began my sales career!)

The great thing about establishing a niche is that it makes it very easy for your target audience to connect with your book because it becomes the obvious choice. On the flip side, a lot of authors fear that if they narrow their focus, they will miss out on sales. But if your book is one of the dozens of general sales guides, how are you going to stand out from the sea of competition? A niche can help you do that and make the whole marketing process a lot easier.

This book, *The Nonfiction Book Marketing Plan*, is written for a specific niche audience. In my case, it has frustrated me for years that book marketing experts speak to all authors, when the needs and goals of nonfiction authors are very different from other authors. I could have simply called this *The Book Marketing Plan*, but I would have missed out on that "aha!" moment that nonfiction authors have when they see the title, plus this book would have ended up in an already crowded category. Worst of all, the contents of the book would have to be diluted in order to accommodate marketing tactics for fiction, children's books, and poetry writers. A niche makes perfect sense for me and helps me connect directly with my ideal target audience.

Oh, and by the way, I can guarantee you that though this book is for nonfiction authors, many authors from other genres will pick it up in hopes of finding some new ideas (and they will). A niche doesn't necessarily prevent others from reading your work, but it speaks directly to those you want to reach. My niche also aligns with my business, my personal goals, and my life experience.

Here are some examples of niches for books:

- Financial guide targeted toward divorced women
- Holistic health book for people living with Diabetes
- Memoir for horse lovers
- European travel guide for retirees
- Cookbook for dairy-free desserts
- Parenting guide for single moms

Can you see how this could work for you? Even if your book isn't targeted toward a specific niche now, you can begin by *marketing to a specific niche audience*. This doesn't mean that you can't serve people outside of your niche, but it does give you a clear focus so you can then develop marketing tactics to meet the specific needs of your target audience.

To determine your niche focus, start by evaluating your readers. Are there any commonalities that they share? Are there themes from your book that have special appeal with a specific kind of audience? Do you have personal experience with a specific audience? Most importantly, pick a market that is narrow enough to be a niche, but not so narrow that the focus is too small.

I cannot stress this point enough, and it's one of the biggest mistakes I see authors make. *If you don't have a clearly defined audience, it will be exceedingly difficult to sell books.*

Build Your Marketing Plan

The first thing you should know about your book is that you need to treat it like a business. Though I know a lot of entrepreneurs will read this book and you probably already understand this, if you are an author with a day job or you're retired and you think you aren't an entrepreneur, I have news for you: You are! Your book is going to generate sales, and if you're generating revenues, you are a business owner.

So now that you realize you have a business, you need to act like a business owner. Most successful entrepreneurs have goals and plans. Most important of all, you need a marketing plan (which is why you're reading this book!). Marketing plans come in many shapes and sizes. My favorite way to create one is by developing a list of marketing tactics and then working through that list over a period of time. Following is an example of a marketing plan template. You can download a copy of this document, which includes multiple worksheets and tabs in an Excel spreadsheet, to help with your planning efforts: http://nonfictionauthorsassociation.com/book-downloads/.

MARKETING TACTICS

TACTIC	DESCRIPTION/TASKS	COST	PRIORITY 1-5	TARGET COMPLETION DATE

As you read through this book you will build your plan, adding tactics that you want to implement. My hope is that you will follow most of the advice in this book while you also come up with some of your own strategies. Know that you don't have to do it ALL, but you do have to find what works for you.

Another important point to remember is that to successfully market anything, a book or a business, you should have multiple concurrent marketing campaigns running at any given time. If your sole book marketing strategy is to set up book signing events at local bookstores, you are going to miss out on a multitude of other effective tactics. So as you build your plan, commit to as many marketing actions as you can handle.

Important Questions to Consider When Building Your Marketing Plan

As you go through the process of building your marketing plan, take time to answer the following questions. You may need to revisit these several times as you read this book. These questions are included in the Book Marketing Action Plan document, which you can download here: http://nonfictionauthorsassociation.com/book-downloads/.

- Who is my ideal target audience? (Age, gender, occupation, location, income level, and other distinguishing factors.)

- What are the biggest challenges for my audience?

- How can I help with each of those challenges? (Whether with my book or with marketing efforts like blogging, professional speaking, etc.)

- Where does my target audience spend their time? (List trade associations, groups, publications they read, websites they visit, events they attend, and any other ways you can reach them.)

- What do I hope readers will take away from my book?

- Describe my book in THREE sentences.

- Describe my book in ONE sentence.

- What marketing tactics have worked well so far? (Hint: Do more of those.)

- What marketing tactics haven't worked?

- How solid is my social media presence?

- What are the top three to five products or services that my readers ask for that I don't yet offer?

- How could I offer those products/services? (Create them myself, refer to others, etc.)

- Rate my website on a scale from 1 to 10.

- What improvements should be made to the site?

- Is it time for a site redesign?

- Does the site have a call to action on the book sales page?

- Is it optimized for the search engines?

- Does it include a blog that is updated a minimum of once per week?

- What is my sales goal for the book for the year?

- What are some ways I can use my book to generate more revenue or business opportunities?

- What is my marketing budget for the year?

- What are my top goals for the business in the coming year?

- What steps do I need to take to reach those goals?

AUTHOR TIP: If you didn't realize until now that you are a business owner, contact an accountant right away. If you establish your business properly (obtain a business license and choose a structure such as sole proprietor, LLC, or S-Corp), you can actually gain some great tax advantages from your home-based business, even if you also have a day job. You should be able to write off many of the expenses involved in publishing and marketing your book! It's not as complicated as it sounds so see an accountant and discuss your options.

Set a Marketing Budget

Most big companies dedicate 10% to 15% of their annual revenues to marketing. As an author—and a business owner—a marketing budget is essential. You'll find many tactics throughout this book that won't cost you a penny beyond your personal time (which, by the way, you should also put a price on). But if you're serious about marketing your book successfully, then you really should dedicate funds to marketing.

This number will be different for every author, and will depend on your goals and revenue potential. It's hard for authors to justify the costs of marketing because the return on investment through book sales alone can be disproportionate. But if you're also marketing your business or using your book to reach bigger goals, then a larger marketing budget makes sense and can produce a greater return on investment (ROI).

I can't tell you how much you should personally budget. However, you should have a better idea after reading through this book and identifying the top marketing tactics you want to employ.

Build Your Brand as an Authority in Your Field

Most nonfiction authors have a unique opportunity to establish themselves as authorities in their fields. So if you've authored a book on leadership for government employees, your goal should be to get known in that field and with that target audience. When a government conference is coming up, you want to be an obvious choice to be a speaker at that event. You also want your blog and social media efforts and everything you do online and offline to appeal to that audience.

Your book may also be an extension of your business, working in concert with your other marketing efforts to attract consulting clients, speaking engagements, corporate sponsors, and other opportunities. To get the best results, you should begin to build a brand for yourself as an authority in your field.

You've already learned the importance of identifying your niche audience, which is the foundation for establishing your brand. Next, everything you do should convey what your brand is about. That means that your marketing collateral, website, business cards, PowerPoint presentations, etc. should all have a consistent message and design. But building a brand involves more than developing a consistent look and feel for your marketing collateral. Here are some important questions to answer:

- What are your core values? In other words, what is important to you in how you run your business and present it to the world? (Remember, authors are entrepreneurs.)

- How do you want your brand to make people feel? (i.e. Strong, empowered, happy, grateful, healthy, hopeful, etc.)

- What kind of tone do you want to set? Should it be professional? Funny? Spiritual? Authoritative?

- What do you want to be known for?

- Can you create a tagline that explains what you're about in seven words or less? (Example: My personal tagline is "Helping business professionals establish authority online.")

- Does your book title or subtitle connect with your target audience?
- Do you need to update your PowerPoint presentations to align with your brand and values?
- Does your website reflect all of the above?
- What marketing collateral needs to be updated? (Business cards, bookmarks, postcards, speaker sheets, flyers, etc.)
- Do you have a consistent color scheme and does it accurately reflect your goals and vision? You can find a great list of colors and their meanings here: http://crystal-cure.com/color-meanings.html.

To continue building your brand, here is a checklist of steps you may need to take:

- Spend some time searching for other authors online to study their branding strategies. Note what you like and don't like as you begin to shape your own strategy.
- Update or redesign your website.
- Write dazzling website copy that speaks to your target audience.
- Revise outdated marketing materials.
- Hire a talented graphic designer to create a consistent look and feel.
- Write a new bio that reflects your brand—one that can be used on your website, in book promotion materials, for speaking engagements, etc.
- Develop a signature speech.
- Write blog posts that compliment your brand goals.
- Build a social media presence that reflects your brand.
- When opportunities come to you, decide whether or not they fit with your brand. (I recently turned down a speaking engagement with a group that didn't align with my personal goal of being authentic online—this was empowering!)
- Consider your brand before writing your next book.

Set Up Google Alerts

One of my favorite free services is Google Alerts (http://alerts.google.com), an Internet monitoring service that sends email notification when keywords or phrases you identify appear online. This service is a goldmine for authors because it allows you to track mentions of your work, mentions of your competitors, and monitor your reputation. Here are some types of Google Alerts you can create:

- **Author Name** – Track mentions of your name online.

- **Website URLs** – Create alerts for your website and/or blog. Note that you can leave off "www" or "http" and simply create the alert for "mywebsite.com."

- **Book Titles** – Whether you have one book or twenty titles, track mentions of your book online with an alert for each. This gives you the opportunity to thank reviewers and others who mention your work. You may also want to write a blog post for your own blog and link back to any major media mentions.

- **Industry Statistics** – Depending on the subject matter of your book, create alerts to track what's happening in the industry. For example, if your book is about small business financing, you might have alerts for "business loan statistics," "angel investing," etc. When you're alerted to new statistics, you can use them to write a relevant blog post, share on social media, or as fodder to create a new PR campaign. Sharing statistics and then providing supporting data or tips can be a great way to capture media attention and build credibility with your audience.

- **Competing Titles/Authors** – It never hurts to keep an eye on the competition. If a competing author lands an interview with a major media outlet, see if you can follow up on that with a slightly different perspective.

- **Speaking Opportunities** – If you speak on the topic of healthy living, create an alert for "call for speakers health" or "health conference" or "healthy living trade show." This takes some creative testing, but can bring you some valuable opportunities.

- **Blogs and News** – Staying on top of news for your industry is a great way to learn and get engaged with your target audience. Create alerts that lead you to news stories, whether from major media sites or blogs. Then, take time to comment on related stories. And don't just say, "Nice article!" Instead, demonstrate your expertise and contribute to the conversation. Add a missing tip that the writer didn't include. Make it interesting and valuable and readers will notice. Also, look for sites that you can potentially write for.

Hire Help

There are many things you can do to run your author business on a shoestring, though there are some investments you can't afford to skip.

Professional Editor – Nothing is more important than having your book professionally edited. It's fine to have it reviewed by a friend or relative, or by teachers and people with English degrees (I hear this a lot), but you still need a professional editor to put the finishing touches on your work. And I can guarantee that even though your highly credentialed friend reviewed your manuscript, the editor will still find errors. Professional editors follow industry style guides to make sure your work is consistent and clean. They review every sentence carefully. Someone doing you a favor isn't likely to look that closely. Professional editing is one of the best investments you can make in producing your book.

Graphic Designer – Homemade book covers, postcards, flyers and other marketing collateral always *look* homemade. If you want to be taken seriously as an author and business professional, find a good graphic designer for your professional design needs. And when it comes to your book cover, make sure you work with a designer who has experience with producing covers. This is a unique skill set, and an experienced designer can make a significant difference.

Website Designer – A template site is fine if that is all you can afford, but it will never compare to a site designed by a pro. More importantly, having access to a professional website designer you can call when you want to change something on your site, or when something goes wrong, can provide a nice level of security and save you a lot of time and heartache. If you're not broke, have your site professionally designed!

Virtual Assistant – Very few authors have a lot of spare time to focus on marketing their books, because most of us also have jobs. That's where a good virtual assistant comes in handy. You can hire someone to help with some of the workload, and manage tasks like research, contacting bloggers, mailing out your books, and other administrative tasks. You can find virtual assistants through http://authorsassistants.com/ and the International Virtual Assistants Association at http://ivaa.org/.

Additional Hires to Consider:

Marketing Support – If you're struggling with marketing your books, consider hiring the help you need. There are many types of marketing services available for authors to help you with marketing planning, online campaigns, social media, and more. (Shameless self-promotion alert! My company, Authority Publishing, provides social media marketing services for authors. http://AuthorityPublishing.com)

Publicist – A publicist is one of the most expensive options for authors so you have to weigh this choice carefully. Publicists typically expect a monthly retainer fee of $2,500 or more. However, an experienced publicist already has relationships with many media professionals, and can help you get the exposure you need. If you want to go big with your book marketing campaign, hiring a publicist can help you do that.

Bookkeeper – Depending on the volume of sales you manage, a professional bookkeeper can help you not only stay sane, but will comply with tax laws that you may not even know about. I recommend hiring a bookkeeper who is also a certified tax planner, and doing so as soon as possible.

Develop Marketing Collateral

There are a few pieces of marketing collateral that every author should have, and many others that are optional. Decide which of these you need:

- **Business Card** – A client recently asked me if he should add the title of "Author" to his business card. Abso-freaking-lutely! You have earned this title. There is also no law against combining titles on a card, such as "CEO, Author." I personally like to see an author's photo and book cover on a business card, too. For my card, my mug is on the front, and book covers are on the back. I also upgraded to fold-over cards so the inside includes tips from my book, and people often comment on those. Make it easy for people to remember you!

- **Postcards** – As a marketer, postcards are one of my favorite pieces of marketing collateral. They are inexpensive to print, recipients don't need to open an envelope to see them, and they are easy to tuck into a book or hand out at an event. For my personal postcards, I have book covers on the front with a few selected testimonials. On the back side I feature a brief bio, details about the books, and contact information. I leave space on the right for mailing. I often use that extra blank space to jot a note and then tuck a postcard into a book before shipping or in a matching envelope and use it for personal stationary. Postcards can be quite versatile.

- **Bookmarks** – Many authors like to create matching bookmarks for books, though these aren't mandatory (I personally prefer postcards). But they are fun and inexpensive and a great way to be memorable with your readers.

- **Speaker Sheet** – If you want to break in to professional speaking, you may want to develop a promotional one-sheet to give to potential contacts. This is discussed further in Chapter 9.

- **Flyers** – Similar to a postcard, you can develop promotional flyers for your books.

- **Tchotchkes** – Some authors like to give away small items to readers. This usually involves having a basket on your display table while signing books or at a trade show. These are entirely optional, and can certainly increase your budget, but they can also be fun. When I was promoting one of my previous books, *LEAP! 101 Ways to Grow Your Business*, I took a basket of frog merchandise to events (the book features a frog on the cover). They were kitschy and fun and generated a lot of smiles at my table. I also printed up buttons with a catchy slogan and handed them out at a big trade show event. That generated a lot of buzz, and I occasionally hear from someone who says, "I still have that button you handed out!"

Resources for printing materials: <u>http://vistaprint.com</u>, <u>http://iprint.com</u>, <u>http://nextdayflyers.com</u>, and <u>http://affordablebuttons.com</u>.

Designate Files for Clips and Victories

As you step up the efforts to market your books, it's a good idea to track your progress beyond sales numbers. There will be many other causes for celebration: when you land a media interview, when you're invited to speak at a big industry event, when you write an article for a trade publication, or when your book receives a nice review on a blog. Do yourself a favor and keep track of these victories, large and small.

Start a binder to keep your "clips," which are cutouts or printouts of media mentions. Also keep track of accomplishments with either a spreadsheet, a simple list on a Word document, or on slips of paper you tuck into a jar. At the end of each year you will begin to see that you've made a lot more progress than you realized.

Recently, a past client called to tell me that after following my advice for years, publishing several books and blogging consistently, he received a phone call inviting him to host his own radio show with a local radio station! These are the kinds of victories you may not see immediately, but can come over time. Incidentally, he is featured in one of the author interviews in this book (Andrew Rogerson).

Ebooks are Not Optional (and Vice Versa)

One question I'm asked often is whether or not I think it's important to have an ebook edition for a book. The answer is almost always an emphatic *Yes*. The ebook market has exploded in recent years. If your book is in print, I can assure you that you will miss out on readers if you don't also have it in ebook format. Many authors will tell you that their ebook sales keep pace with, or even exceed, their print book sales.

I will admit that I am a convert. I'm also a former bookstore owner and die hard book lover. For many years I have taken pride in filling many shelves in my home with hundreds of books. But then I discovered the joys of reading on the Kindle and iPad. I can get on a plane with a whole library of reading choices and no longer have to stuff my suitcase full of books. Today, when I want to buy a new book, I always check to see if it's available in Kindle format first. Many of your readers are doing the same thing.

The only time that an ebook doesn't make sense is when your book is more like a workbook. Ebook readers can't write in an ebook. However, you can always convert a workbook to an ebook and then offer readers a downloadable PDF for the worksheets.

And by the way, the reverse is also true. If you've published in ebook format only, you are likely missing out on sales since a large part of the population still prefers to hold a book in their hands. A printed book is also tangible. You can't autograph an ebook and it's difficult, though not impossible, to sell them at the back of the room for speaking engagements (some people handle this by providing a postcard with a coupon code to download the ebook, but this can be confusing for readers who are technophobes). If you care about attracting media coverage, then a printed book is essential because most media professionals believe that you must have a printed book to call yourself an author.

Bottom line: format your book as an ebook, too. It's inexpensive to do, and will help you reach far more readers.

How to Land on The New York Times Best Sellers List

Most authors would love nothing more than to have their books appear on *The New York Times* Best Seller list. This list is the Holy Grail for authors—the ultimate sign of success. But the long-standing challenge for self-published authors has been that the list is compiled based on brick and mortar bookstore sales, and most self-published authors aren't featured in bookstores unless they are working with a distributor. Without bookstore distribution (combined with a heck of a lot of promotion), it's impossible for a self-published book to make it to the list.

For those with traditionally published books, your chances are much greater. However, the best sellers list is compiled based on in-store sales from across the country, and not all stores are included in the reporting. To make it to the list, you have to sell thousands of books across hundreds of stores in the same week. This is most likely to happen if you have a major media campaign and land on one of the morning news shows or a big talk show. You might also be able to accomplish this by getting booked for dozens of interviews on radio shows and in print publications.

The good news is that *The New York Times* also features a best sellers list for ebooks, which is compiled based on sales reported from Amazon, Barnes and Noble, Apple, and Google. If you distribute your ebook through these channels and achieve exceptional sales, you can absolutely make it to this list.

Still don't believe it's possible? In 2012, independent ebook distributor Smashwords announced that four of its authors were featured on *The New York Times* Best Seller List *in the same week.* This was BIG news for all self-published authors because it provided evidence of what is possible when you produce your book and then commit to marketing it consistently! We'll explore ebook marketing tactics in chapter 8.

Get Big Name Endorsements for Your Book

In the weeks before your book is published, you should begin reaching out to fellow authors to request endorsements. Ideally, testimonials should come from *authors* in your field, and the more well-known the author, the better. And while you may think that big-name authors are untouchable, think again. Smart authors know that endorsing a book enhances their marketing efforts since they gain added visibility with your readers. And the fact is that it never hurts to ask. All they can do is say no, but they just might surprise you and say yes!

The key to getting the attention of well-known authors is to show up like a pro. Avoid telling them your whole life story and never beg or suck up. Also, avoid ranting about how this is your first book, you're self-publishing, and you have no idea if anyone will ever buy your work—that will NOT inspire good results!

Contact information for even the biggest authors is almost always available. Search their websites or reach out via social media mail. You'd be surprised by who reads their own mail on Facebook and LinkedIn!

Endorsement requests should be short and sweet. Authors are busy and don't have time to read a two-page pitch. A brief endorsement request will also make you look like a pro. Here's a sample that you can model and send out via email:

> Hi <author name>,
>
> I enjoyed your book <title> and found it enlightening because…
> <briefly explain>
>
> I have a new book coming out this winter: <title> (published by
> <publishing company name>). It is about <brief description, just two
> or three sentences>. I am in the process of gathering endorsements

for the jacket. Would you consider providing a testimonial? I would be happy to send you sample chapters or the entire manuscript for review—whichever you prefer.

Thanks very much for your consideration!

Warm wishes,

<your name>
<contact information and website link>
<social media links if you have an impressive following>

Note that this letter starts out by complimenting the author's work. This demonstrates that you are a fan of their work and creates an instant rapport (flattery will get you everywhere!). Mentioning the publishing company also adds credibility *unless you are using one of the* <u>big box self-publishing houses</u>. If that's the case, omit the publishing company information. The unfortunate reality is that inexpensive publishing solutions will be recognizable and an author with a major press behind him will not be impressed. Also, write two or three of the most compelling sentences you can muster about your book and why it is great.

What Happens After You Reach Out

You can expect to receive responses within a few days. Some authors may ask for the full manuscript, though most simply want to see a table of contents and a few sample chapters so they know you can write. The vast majority will not take time to read your book from cover to cover. Do not take this personally!

Some may ask for you to send over some sample testimonials. That's right, they will ask you to write a few examples that they can choose from! They may change a word or two around, but for the most part you will be crafting your own endorsement. This is a reality in this business.

The bottom line is that endorsements do enhance the credibility of a book, so don't be afraid to pursue them with gusto. Make a list of ten to twenty authors and start asking. With any luck, you'll end up with so many testimonials that you'll need to add a page or two to the beginning of your book to accommodate them!

Trade Associations and Conferences

As an author, it can be beneficial to connect with other authors so that you can learn from each other and help each other succeed. Start by looking for a local authors and publishers group. Start with a Google search, ask at your local bookstore or library, and search events on http://Craigslist.org and http://meetup.com. Most major metro areas should have a professional authors' association.

On a national level, I recommend the Independent Book Publishers Association (http://ibpa-online.org), which publishes an excellent monthly magazine and hosts online events and a fabulous annual conference.

While I've been writing this book, I have been in the process of launching the Nonfiction Authors Association, which is conducted completely online: http://NonfictionAuthorsAssociation.com. Be sure to stop by and set up a free author profile, and also consider joining us for ongoing marketing education and to be part of a supportive community of fellow authors.

Writer's conferences can also be beneficial for learning and meeting industry professionals. You can find a comprehensive list of events at http://writing.shawguides.com/. I will add that for years I have found it frustrating that most writer's conferences and groups forget about nonfiction authors. Instead, there is a heavy emphasis on fiction writers, followed by children's book writers. Because of this, in 2010 I launched the first online conference specifically for nonfiction authors: http://NonfictionWritersConference.com.

Author Interview

Name: Dan Poynter

Websites: http://ParaPublishing.com, http://GlobalEbookAwards.com, http://ParaPromotion.com, and others

Books:

- *Dan Poynter's Self-Publishing Manual: How to Write, Print and Sell Your Own Book*
- *Dan Poynter's Self-Publishing Manual: How to Write, Print and Sell Your Own Book (Volume 2)*

- *Writing Nonfiction: Turning Thoughts into Books*
- *Parachuting: The Skydiver's Handbook*
- *Book Fairs: An Exhibiting Guide for Publishers*
- *Book Publishing Encyclopedia*
- *Successful Nonfiction: Tips and Inspiration for Getting Published*
- *The Expert Witness Handbook: Tips and Techniques for the Litigation Consultant*
- *Is There a Book Inside You?: Writing Alone or with a Collaborator*
- *The Parachute Manual : A Technical Treatise on Aerodynamic Decelerators (Vol. 2)*
- *The Older Cat: Recognizing Decline & Extending Life*
- *Write & Grow Rich: Using Voice-Recognition to Dictate Your How-To-Book*
- *U-Publish.com: How 'U' Can Compete with the Giants of Publishing*

Are you traditionally published or self-published, and why did you make that choice?

Both. I have sold out to major publishers in the US and abroad (foreign rights). I have published other authors, and have published myself; 132 books at all.

Tell us a bit about your most recent book.

My first work of fiction. Rusty Martin is born to an aviation family and grows up in Casselberry, Florida, in the 1930s. He is 12 at the outbreak of WW-II. Flying takes the young man to many fascinating events of the time.

You will discover:

- Many significant events in 1939 through 1943.
- The stories behind the stories.
- What aviation was like in the 30's & 40's.
- An inspirational story that could have happened.

■ How much more exciting fiction can be with pictures, maps and video.

This is a work of historical fiction and it is a new type of fiction: the ebook is illustrated. Most of the places, events, and people are real. Much of the dialogue is presumed. The main character is fictional—but could be real.

This book describes an interesting time and celebrates the people who lived it. If they did not say and do some of the things described, I hope they would agree that they could have.

Fascinating, inspirational, educational, and a great read. You will love following Rusty's adventures.

This ebook is a multimedia presentation. Employing maps, photographs, videos, audios, and written references, this enhanced ebook can tell a story in a way that a print book cannot. Most of the photographs and videos in this book are in black and white. That is because they are circa 1940. I have done my best to be faithful to history—to show and describe events and places as they were.

Read this novel on an e-reading device (Kindle, Nook, iPad, etc.) that is connected to the Internet to take full advantage of this enhanced ebook.

Readers may find some of the incidents described difficult to believe. The references testify to the ebook's accuracy. The main character in this novel is Rusty Martin. He is reasonably smart, and very resourceful. Most of all, he is in the right places at the right times.

As Rusty would tell you, life is a moving target. To be successful, you should see what is going on and look to the future. Life is never as it used to be and it will never again be as it is now. Times will change and with change comes opportunity. Rusty reads, Rusty listens, Rusty studies, Rusty learns, and Rusty acts.

Aviation is in our future though much of the Army and Navy leadership resisted the thought in the 1920s, 1930s, and even into the 1940s.

President Roosevelt, on the other hand, saw aviation in the future. If you are old enough to have been in these places during the times discussed, and if you have additional or corrected information, please contact me. This book is a growing work. It will be updated from time to time. Books reflect on their authors and this author wants this ebook to reflect positively.

With your help, the readership of this book will climb like a homesick angel.

Who is your target audience of readers?
Most of my books are written for authors and publishers. A number of my books are written for skydivers and aviators. I also have specialized books on other individual subjects from word processors (1981) to Frisbee Play (1977).

What has been the single most effective marketing strategy you have used for promoting your book?
That depends upon what year the book was published because the industry is constantly evolving. Today it is book bloggers—on your book's subject. The book bloggers have numerous subscribers who are dedicated to and focused on your book's subject.

What are some other marketing tactics that have or haven't worked for you?
Borders is gone. Barnes & Noble is closing brick-and-mortar stores. The independent bookstores are difficult to reach. The new reality is Amazon. com. Authors should deal directly with Amazon, update their profile, and promote reviews at Amazon.

Traditional book reviewers are almost gone. Pursue the book bloggers on your subject.

How has social media impacted your success? Which social media networks do you feel generate the best results for you?

Take part in the forums and groups at Yahoo, LinkedIn, and so on. Learn from the questions and answers and answer when you can. Whenever you answer a question, sign it with your name, your book title, and your website

URL. As the author of a book, you are an expert; your book provides additional credibility.

What have been some of the biggest benefits of publishing a book?
Credibility in the subject area of your book. Authors are author-ities and the public perceives authors and books in high esteem.

What advice would you offer to new authors who are getting ready to promote their books?
The most expensive parts of book promotion are the mistakes. You do not have to make them. Attend the conventions, take part in groups and forums, purchase the books, get a Book Shepherd, et cetera. Get as much information as possible.

If you were starting over today, is there anything you would you do differently?
That would depend on when I started. Back in 1969 it was a different book trade. Each year situations that evolved. What worked years ago does not work today. Today book promotion is faster, easier and cheaper due to the Internet. People anywhere in the world can find you, your book, and your subject with a simple Internet search. And you can find buyers for your book in the world's largest library – the Internet.

Chapter 2:
Launch a Killer Website

*"The internet is becoming the town square
for the global village of tomorrow."*
— Bill Gates

WHEN DEVELOPING A WEBSITE to promote your book, you have two primary choices: You can launch a site for the book (booktitle.com) or for you as the author (authorname.com). Between the two, my recommendation is almost always to develop an author website instead of a book site.

If your goal is to brand yourself as an authority in your field, professional speaker or media interview source, it makes sense to focus efforts on developing your personal brand, with your book being an extension of that brand. Maintaining an author site also makes it easier to manage if you intend to write additional books in the future.

Of course you can still have a separate book site if you really want to, and some authors prefer this strategy. However, I personally prefer to focus my efforts on updating and promoting one primary site and driving all of the traffic to that specific site.

There is also a third option that you may not have considered: launch an industry site. This is an approach I took in 2004 with my first book, *The Business Startup Checklist and Planning Guide*. I wanted to reach aspiring entrepreneurs and so I launched an industry site (http://BusinessInfoGuide.com) and loaded it with content for that audience. I wrote articles, shared resources, and basically began blogging before I knew what blogging was. The site was live for about nine months before my book came out, which gave me time to build an audience. When I listed the book for pre-sale two months before it was actually in print, it began selling immediately. That was when I really understood the power of using the Internet to build an audience.

Over the years the site has evolved and grown exponentially. Not only has it helped me establish my authority in the small business space, it has also been a steady revenue generator. It has earned money from advertising placed on the site and it's also attracted numerous corporate sponsors. It's a venue for me to promote new books, events, and products, and has attracted a tremendous amount of media coverage over the years. In the early years I produced all of the content on the site, but today we feature guest articles and interviews by other contributors.

Another example of an industry site is SparkPeople.com, which is a weight loss community filled with articles and message boards for its members. Founder Chris Downie wrote a book for his audience: *The Spark: The 28-Day Breakthrough Plan for Losing Weight, Getting Fit, and Transforming Your Life.* Because he had a built-in audience, the book quickly hit the best sellers lists. His team has since launched several subsequent books.

So if you wrote a book about elder care, you could launch a site loaded with resources for families dealing with aging parents. If your book is a guide for parents of teenagers, your site could cater to the joys and trials of raising hormonal monsters (I mean kids). If you're a relationship coach and author, you could host a site that shares marriage tips.

In case you're wondering, this also means that you might actually launch two websites. I also maintain a separate author site at http://StephanieChandler. com. My author site is primarily used to attract speaking engagements and media interviews, yet it's another source for traffic and book sales.

One final option is to launch an industry guide within your main website domain. Annie Jennings PR recently launched an online magazine, which is hosted under the main business domain: http://anniejenningspr. com/jenningswire/. This model can be a great way to drive traffic to your main website, while also filling your site with content that appeals to your target audience. It also gives you a reason to enlist guest contributors, and those folks can help to promote your site and reach an even bigger audience.

Author Websites: How to Make Yours Rock!

Following are some basic pages to consider when planning your website:

Home Page – A brief overview about you and your book. Make it interesting, fun, engaging and different! Note that your home page can also feature your recent blog posts, but only do this if you are committed to blogging several times each week.

About the Author – This should include an interesting bio about you and your qualifications for writing your book(s). Spice it up with some professional photos. Keep it fresh and interesting by showing some personality here.

Media – A media page is a great place to showcase any media coverage you have received. Be sure to list all media outlets, including print, radio and television. Also, make it easy for media pros to cover you for a story. Include short and extended bios, plus high resolution, professional photos that can be downloaded by media pros. Over time the goal should be to fill this page with lots of impressive media logos.

Speaker – If you speak about topics related to your book—or if you want to speak—include a speaker page. List your speaking topics along with a description of what is covered. Include testimonials from past engagements and a list of any audiences that you've spoken to. It's also a good idea to include a printable single-page speaker sheet that can be downloaded in PDF format.

Contact – Your contact page should provide a way for visitors to email you directly. Web contact forms are fine, but also include an email link since some prefer that. Also, include a phone number and physical mailing address. Never use your home address! Treat your book like a business and invest in a mailbox from The UPS Store or your local post office. If you work with a publicist or assistant, you can also include their contact information here.

Blog – Every author needs a blog. Here is where you can share topics related to your book, quick tips, excerpts from the book, recipes and anything else your target audience will enjoy. Update your blog at least twice each week (more is better). Over time your blog will bring more traffic to your site. It also becomes the heart of your social media efforts. Keep reading for more on the important topic of blogging.

Sidebar and Navigation – Some elements should be visible across your entire website. Include links to your social media profiles and a sign-up box for your mailing list. If your site is built on WordPress, there are some great plug-ins you can include such as Recent Tweets, which will display your Twitter feed. You can also feature your book, recent blog posts or announcements.

Photos and Video – If you have photos or videos to share, your website is a great place to showcase them. They can be featured on their own pages, within the existing pages on your site or in your blog. Google loves sites that feature videos and other media so this can only assist in helping your site generate more traffic.

Services – If you offer services related to your book, such as coaching or consulting, be sure to list them here.

Products – If you offer companion products, such as videos, audio recordings, workbooks, or templates, add either a "Products" page or a "Store" page.

Create a Web Sales Page for Your Book

The sales page for your book is extremely important. It should attract visitors and entice them to buy. Here are the elements to include on your sales page:

1. **Detailed Description of Your Book** – This could be information from your book jacket or an expanded version of your jacket copy. Either way, it should be written to entice readers. Marketing copy should focus on the *benefits* for the reader and explain why they should read your book—not just an overview of what the book is about. What problems does your book solve? That's the kind of information potential readers need to know.

2. **Author Bio and Photo** – Even if you have an extended bio on another page of your site, be sure to include a brief bio so that visitors who don't take the time to poke around other pages will get an immediate answer about who you are and why you wrote the book. Include a photo since this helps them identify with you.

3. **Book Cover Image** – This may sound obvious, but this is a big mistake I see on a lot of sites. The cover image may already be included in the website header so authors think it doesn't need to be included again. Wrong! If you or your readers share a link to your book on Facebook, for example, you will want to make sure it can display with a preview of the cover image—and that won't be possible if it's part of the website header.

4. **Testimonials** – If you have them, use them. Testimonials are social proof that your work is good and can help improve sales. If you don't have any, then go get some!

5. **Sample Reading** – There are a number of ways to approach this. I like to include a PDF version of the table of contents from my book. Some authors give away a sample chapter or two as a free download. If you do this, I'd suggest requiring sign up for your mailing list so you can reach that potential buyer again later.

6. **Purchase Link(s)** – Make it as easy as possible for visitors to purchase your book by offering one or more link options for purchase. If you're shipping your books yourself, it can be as simple as setting up a PayPal button. If you don't want to ship books (and it's totally fine if that is the case), then make sure you offer a link to purchase on Amazon and/or other online booksellers. And don't forget your ebooks. If you're offering an ebook version of your book, add a purchase link to Amazon's Kindle store or Smashwords or whatever service you're using. I also like to sell a PDF version of my book from my site. It's remarkable how many people buy them, and if they're savvy, they know how to load a PDF up on their Kindle, Nook or iPad.

7. **Consider Bonus Items** – Some authors host campaigns to give away a bunch of bonus items "if you buy the book today only!" The truth is that these campaigns are not my favorite because the results are usually temporary. So here's another approach: offer bonus items for the first month—or the whole year and beyond! Why not make it irresistible for potential buyers? You can compile a list of bonuses from your own files (such as special reports, spreadsheets, templates, audio recordings, etc.), or you can ask peers to contribute bonus items. Many will be happy to do so as a way for them to get exposure with your audience.

8. **Social Sharing Buttons** – As a general rule for websites and blogs, all pages should have social media sharing buttons for Facebook, Twitter, LinkedIn, Google+, Pinterest, etc. Depending on your website platform, these are usually easy to add. I like the ShareThis widget for WordPress.

My last bit of advice: Keep it simple. Website visitors have short attention spans. You don't need big, bold headlines to sell a book. You need really great sales copy that makes a reader think, "I need this book!"

And by the way, you can set up a pre-sale offer for your book several weeks or even months prior to its release. All you really need to do this is a shopping cart button, which you can create with http://paypal.com. Make sure you are fairly certain about the release date and let early buyers know when to expect their shipment. You can entice them to buy in advance by offering a discount, personally autographed copies, or a bonus to go along with the book (like an extra report or audio download).

Search Engine Optimization Basics

Search Engine Optimization (SEO) is what you do to improve your website's organic ranking with the search engines (Google, Yahoo, Bing, etc.). Since around 70% of Internet searches are conducted with Google, it's a good idea to focus on how Google ranks your site. Google uses complex algorithms to determine a website's relevance and its ranking when a search is conducted. And though Google has recently made some significant changes to the way it serves up search results (more emphasis on local results and sites you've previously interacted with), you can still get Google's attention by following some basic SEO principles.

Why Text Matters

Google uses technology called spiders to "crawl" across web pages, looking for patterns in the text (keyword concentration). This is one of the ways it determines what a website offers and how it should be categorized. It is the most basic and perhaps the most important element in gaining better placement in search engines.

Every web page has a place to indicate the keywords, page title and description. This information gets encoded in the page and is the first data that Google sees. When this data is absent or unfocused, it can hurt your site's relevance with Google.

Using Keywords

Keywords should include individual words and phrases that your target audience would most likely use to locate you or your book. For example, if you're an author of a book on business financing and you're also a speaker, your key phrases might look like this:

- Author business financing book

- Author <your name>

- Professional speaker <your name>

- Book <book title>

- Professional speaker San Francisco

- Professional speaker California

- Professional speaker business financing

- Business loans

- Business consulting loans

- Consultant business financing

- Business loan consultant San Francisco

To locate keyword suggestions, hop on over to Google's free keyword tool (https://adwords.google.com/o/KeywordTool). When you type in a phrase, it will return results for similar phrases and will show you how popular each phrase is in searches. You will want to target phrases that have a medium or low popularity since it will be easier to get visibility in search for content with those phrases compared with phrases that have a high level of competition.

Keywords work best when they match the *content* on your web page. So when writing your web copy, it's best to repeat the most important keyword phrase throughout the page two or three times. If you want your page to come up when someone searches for "Dallas leadership consultant," then there should be several mentions of that phrase throughout the text on that page. Also, use the keyword phrase in the first paragraph of text. Google may not crawl all the way down each page so the first two paragraphs are prime real estate.

Of course there is a caveat to all of this. The search engines will penalize you if you try to beat the system. So don't bother repeating keywords dozens of times—Google will view this as keyword stuffing and it could actually hurt your ranking or get your site removed from the search engine altogether. Google does care about keyword density. Good keyword density should add up to 4% to 7% of the content on the page, with 93% of the page for other content.

Ultimately, you will get the best results if you develop a keyword map for your entire site. *Each and every page on your site should have its own unique set of keywords*, which allows you to maximize the potential search traffic. This strategy also means that a standard five-page website isn't enough. If you want to increase the chances of being found in the search engines for numerous sets of keywords, the best way to do that is with numerous pages—one describing each book, product, service, the city where you're located, etc.

Also, keep in mind that it can be far easier to get traffic from Google for a keyword phrase based on a city (also known as local search marketing). If you're a life coach in Boise who has authored a book on work-life balance, your keywords might look like this:

- Life coach Boise
- Work life balance Boise
- Speaker work life balance Boise
- Life coach Idaho
- Author work life balance Boise

Though I'm a big proponent of building a global audience online, don't forget to capture the audience in your own backyard. Include cities in major metro areas nearby, plus smaller cities in your area.

By the way, you don't have to include all of your web pages in your main site navigation. It's fine to create some additional pages for search engine marketing purposes that users would find only through an Internet search.

Page Title

The title for each page is displayed at the top of the browser, in the data returned from an Internet search, and as the description when someone bookmarks the page in their Internet "favorites" folder. I see a lot of sites that simply read "Home" at the top of the page. Don't make this mistake! Be sure to incorporate your keywords for each page into the title.

Page Description

Include a brief description for each web page. This is the information that is listed after the page title when your page shows up in search engine results. Make sure your description includes your keyword phrase.

Page Link

The URL for each web page can also help with placement on Google. For example, the link to the typical "About Us" page might look something like this:

authorwebsite.com/aboutus

A keyword-rich link name can be more effective:

authorwebsite.com/about-joe-author-business-leadership-book

If you are just in the process of setting up your site, you have the opportunity to create keyword-rich links for your pages. If your site is already live, this could be a hassle, but a good web designer can help you make the transition without breaking any existing links on your site.

Photos and Videos

Each photo or video that you add to your site not only adds appeal for the site visitor, but it can assist in your SEO strategy. Images have "alt tags;" a place where you can include a description of the image for the visually impaired or for visitors who are unable to view images online (some corporations and government entities control their employees' Internet access by blocking images from appearing online). Since the search engines don't yet have the capability of interpreting photo images and video the way that they understand text, they look for the alt image tags and descriptions. Take advantage of the added SEO benefit and make sure that every image and video on your site includes an alt image tag with a keyword-rich title.

Also, including a caption below the photo is yet another opportunity to add a description. Studies also show that site visitors are drawn to reading captions placed below photos. For some reason our eyes are drawn there, and this is an opportunity to draw attention to a key message that you want to convey for that page.

Lastly, the actual file name for each image provides yet another opportunity to improve keyword concentration. For example, instead of inserting an image simply named *photo.jpg*, rename the image to something like *corporate-leadership-book-joe-author.jpg*.

Inbound Links

One of the criteria that the search engines use to rank website pages is the number of inbound links pointing to your website from other websites. More importantly, Google looks at how many links from *high-traffic* websites are pointing to your pages. If a popular website features a link to your site, it shows the search engines that your site is important.

Other valuable incoming links are those that come from industry-related sites. When other sites in the same industry link to your site, it can improve your site's relevance with the search engines. So if you're a gardening expert and other websites that discuss gardening point to your site, this will give your site a boost.

Government sites (with a .gov extension) and education sites (with a .edu extension) also have high priority with the search engines. If you're able to get incoming links from any of these sites, it can help your ranking.

Where to Promote Your Website Link:

- Update the free online profiles provided by any trade organizations that you belong to.

- Ask colleagues and business partners to swap links with you. They can publish your link on a "Recommended Resources" or similar page on their site, and you can do the same in return.

- Publish articles on industry websites and include your bio and website link. The more articles you push out across the Internet, the more links you will have pointing back to your site. The same is true for guest blog posts.

- Share specific page links via social media.

- Update online profiles for all sites where you are a member including eBay, Amazon, Yahoo, Google, etc. Take advantage of every opportunity you can find to post your link online.

Some services offer to add lots of inbound links to your site—beware! Adding dozens of links at once can be viewed by the search engines as spam. It takes time to get your link out there, so always be on the lookout for opportunities to generate inbound links.

Anchored Links

An anchored link is a link to a web page that is embedded in text. For example, when "Click here for more information" is an active hyperlink to a Web page, it is an anchored link. Anchored links are a boon for SEO because they tell the search engines what content is found on the linked page. Because of this, links should incorporate keywords instead of the generic "Click here" example.

For example, a high-traffic site with a link embedded in the text saying "Meet Joe Author, author and speaker specializing in business leadership" would be an excellent anchored link.

The hardest part of this strategy is getting others to link back to your site in the first place, and then to do so with an anchored link. But because anchored links are so valuable, it's worth at least asking your link partners to do this whenever possible.

Anchor Pages Throughout Your Site

You can also weave anchored links throughout *your own site* to the different pages within your site. For example, from your home page, you could include a link that says "Find out more about Joe Author's leadership book." When you write a new blog post that refers to a previous blog post that you wrote, add an anchored link to see the previous post.

Other Important SEO Strategies

Following are some additional strategies to incorporate into your SEO plans.

Headline Tags - One important factor in featuring the keywords that are central on your web pages is the use of headline tags. A headline is denoted on a webpage with basic HTML code: <h1>, <h2>, <h3>, etc. These tags not only affect the formatting of the text, but search engines interpret headlines as being important content on a page, so these should include the keywords for the page. Be sure to check with your web designer to see if your headlines are properly coded. Also, note that text in larger fonts or bolded using a <strong> tag will also be noticed by the search engines.

Longevity - Generally speaking, the longer your website is in existence, the better. Newer sites are not regarded as highly by Google as those that have been live for months or years. There's not much you can do about this, but know that your site's standing can improve over time.

Flash - Flash is a special type of code often used to create dynamic elements on pages (such as rotating images). Some websites have a Flash landing page where you must click to proceed to the site's main page. Unfortunately, Flash is not search-engine friendly.

Avoid using a Flash introduction page (the main home page for your site) at all costs as it could block Google from viewing your site. If you use Flash within your site, use it sparingly and be sure to set alt tags that describe the text on the page. It's also a good idea to offer an html-only version of your site to help the search engines and to ensure that web users who can't view flash are still able to view your site. Currently, iPad users cannot see Flash images, and considering there are millions of iPad users today, this can present a challenge. In my opinion, it's best to avoid Flash altogether.

Broken Links - If you feature links to other websites, periodically verify that they are working. If a business closes and the website is shut down and you have a non-functioning link on your site, your ranking can be penalized because Google doesn't like broken links.

Site Redesign - When you completely redesign your site and upload all of the changes at once, prepare to take a hit from Google. Unfortunately, Google doesn't like it when all of a site's pages change at once, but over time you will regain your position. Also, if you do have your site redesigned, make sure you don't break existing page links. If your pages change or are renamed, ask your web designer to set up .htaccess 301 redirects for each changed link.

AUTHOR TIP: Install Google Analytics on your website. This is a free service from Google and provides extensive data about your website traffic, how many page views your site receives, how many unique visitors, which pages get the most traffic, where traffic comes from (referral sources like Twitter), and which keywords bring you the most traffic. Analytics provide essential data and should be installed on your site ASAP. Set up a free account at http://analytics.google.com.

Why Every Author Needs a Blog

I firmly believe that every author needs a blog. Hosting a blog gives you a way to connect with your readers, and it's also incredibly powerful for SEO. The more content you add to your blog, the more reasons you give Google to find your site. You also naturally build up keyword concentration with the topics you write about, bringing even more traffic over time. I learned about the benefits firsthand when I was first running BusinessInfoGuide.com. With each new article I added to the site, the traffic increased.

Content is king, and the more often you update your site, the better. For best results, that means blogging often, so set a goal to update your blog at least two to three times per week. It will take some time to build your audience, but your traffic should increase steadily. And if you think blogging takes too much time, consider this: you're a writer and hosting a blog gives you an opportunity to exercise your writing muscles! I am grateful that I get to blog each week. It reminds me that I am a writer and it's one of my favorite things that I do. It also becomes fodder for my future books. A good portion of this book was born from my blog on AuthorityPublishing.com.

How to Start a Blog

If you don't yet have a blog on your website, contact your webmaster and see if you can add one. Depending on how your site was built, you may be able to add a blog to your existing site. If that's not an option, then consider having your site redesigned. While that may sound like a major undertaking, adding a blog will make it worthwhile in the long run.

If you're starting from scratch, I recommend having your site built on WordPress, which is a powerful blogging platform. Find a web designer who knows how to build sites on WordPress (most should these days).

The last option is to launch a blog on another website, such as blogger. com. However, when you host your blog on a different domain, your main website can't reap the rewards of the increased content and traffic. For best results, your blog should be hosted directly on your primary website domain.

Ways to Increase Blog Traffic and Reader Engagement

Many authors find it frustrating to build an audience by blogging because it typically takes time to build momentum. Following are effective ways to accelerate the process, increase traffic, engage readers, and improve the overall effectiveness of your blog:

1. **Share with Social Media** – Each new blog post that you write should be shared across your social networks, including Facebook, Twitter, LinkedIn, Google+, and Pinterest. Be sure to share the blog title with a link to continue reading on your site. We'll discuss this more in Chapter 3.

2. **Submit Your Blog to Directories** – There are many directories where readers can find your blog. Here are some to get you started:

- http://blogcatalog.com
- http://mybloglog.com
- http://blogflux.com
- http://technorati.com
- http://blogarama.com
- http://blogexplosion.com
- http://bloghub.com
- http://globeofblogs.com
- http://networkedblogs.com
- http://bloghop.com

3. **Promote in Your E-newsletter** – Summarize your recent blog posts in your newsletter by including the title, first paragraph, and a link to keep reading on your site.

4. **Write Captivating Titles** – The most important element of any blog post that you write is a captivating title. You want to hook potential readers so that they will click through to keep reading. Study blog titles on popular blogs to see how they make them more enticing.

5. **Understand Your Audience** – A big missing component for a lot of bloggers is a failure to understand their target audience. Remember that you need to first define *who your audience is* and then *what their challenges are.* Then you can write content that appeals to their needs, challenges, and interests.

6. **Share Your Link** – Make sure your blog link is listed in your online profiles, your bio on social media sites, and in your email signature.

7. **Host Giveaways** – Offer free items from your blog periodically. For example, you could give away a sample chapter from your book or a special report. You could also enlist others to donate items to give away to anyone who leaves a comment.

8. **Hold a Contest** – In addition to frequent giveaways, you can also hold contests where one or more winners are selected. Prizes can include a copy of a book, a brief consultation with you, attendance

at an event you are hosting, a gift card, or anything else your audience would find valuable. You can also enlist other companies to donate prizes.

9. **Increase Blog Frequency** – Studies have shown that site traffic increases exponentially as you add more content to your blog on a consistent basis. Ideally, you should update your blog at least two to three times per week, though remember that more content will lead to more traffic.

10. **Retweet Past Content** – If you have an archive of past blog posts, you can still tweet them out as long as they are still relevant. WordPress users can also install the Tweet Old Post plug-in, which will automatically tweet out your past blog content based on parameters you set.

11. **Feature Guest Contributors** – Invite others to contribute content to your blog, including industry experts and peers. Once their post is featured, ask them to share with their networks. To streamline the process, create submission forms on your site. We invite guest contributors at BusinessInfoGuide.com: http://businessinfoguide.com/directory/contribute/.

12. **Develop Theme Days** – Author Karl Palachuk features "SOP Fridays" on his blog at http://smallbizthoughts.com. His audience knows that each week Karl will share important Standard Operating Procedures for the IT industry (his target audience). This series has been wildly popular, bringing a tremendous amount of traffic each week. Karl also plans to turn the entire series into a book.

13. **Optimize Your Posts** – Make sure to identify a keyword phrase for each blog post and incorporate it into the headline and within the text on the page two or three times.

14. **Include Social Sharing Buttons** – Make it easy for your readers to promote your blog posts by including social media sharing buttons. The major blog platforms each offer free plug-ins for these.

15. **Ask for Comments** – One of the biggest complaints from bloggers is that they don't generate many comments. The vast majority of visitors won't take time to leave a comment, but you can encourage

them to do so by simply asking! At the bottom of each post, ask a question or simply invite readers to respond in the comment box below. It's amazing how this simple request can yield results.

16. **Respond to Comments** – One of the big benefits of a blog is that you can engage with your audience. Respond to all comments and let your audience know you're paying attention, even if you simply say, "Thank you for taking the time to post."

17. **Comment on Other Blogs** – When you write a comment on another blog, you get the opportunity to include your photo, name, and a link back to your own site. Get known within your industry by being a power contributor to other industry blogs. And be sure to leave compelling comments. A good comment contributes to the conversation by adding another tip or expounding on something the blog author mentioned. Provide value and fellow blog readers will find you.

18. **Link to Other Blogs and Websites** – When writing blog posts, add relevant links to any resources that you mention. Not only will readers appreciate this, the companies you mention may also take notice. You might be surprised by how those companies end up referring to your blog in one of their posts.

19. **Include Photos and Graphics** – Images make blog posts more visually appealing to readers, and will make your posts look more professional when shared on social media sites because the photo will appear with the post preview. I strongly recommend adding a photo to every blog post. Make sure to use royalty-free images from a site like Clipart.com. Also, be sure to add a keyword phrase to the alt tag and description to each image to boost SEO.

20. **Cross-Reference Past Content** – When writing new posts, include anchored links to related posts that you've written previously. Links keep readers engaged, and they are also good for search engine optimization across your site.

21. **Feature Related Posts** – At the end of each new blog post, it can be beneficial to mention other blog posts. You can summarize these yourself or WordPress users can install the Yet Another Related Posts plug-in, which will automatically serve up links to related content based on keyword tags.

22. **Write Guest Blog Posts** – Contributing to other blog sites, especially high-traffic sites, can help you build an audience of readers who want to know more about you. Make sure your bio features a link directly back to your blog.

23. **Review Your Site Design** – If you want your blog to be taken seriously, it should be professionally designed, formatted for easy reading, and visually appealing. Look at your blog objectively and compare it with others in your field. When in doubt, ask some professional contacts to give you constructive feedback. Often times a simple redesign can increase readership dramatically.

24. **Do More of What Works** – Pay attention to the activity generated by each of your blog posts, noting which posts get the most traffic, comments, retweets, etc., and which ones fall flat. Do more of what works!

AUTHOR TIP: If you want your photo to appear when you comment on another blog, set up a free profile at https://en.gravatar.com/, which is where many sites automatically collect this information.

How to Add More Content to Your Blog

Whenever I discuss the benefits of blogging, inevitably I hear grumbles and groans from the audience. It seems that many people resist blogging due to the fear that it will take a lot of time. While it's true that blogging can be time-consuming, there are ways to make it easier.

I have been blogging for many years now, and it's truly one of my favorite things that I do each week. There was also a time when I would occasionally get stricken with "blogger's block" (the equivalent of writer's block). So here are some ways you can add more content to your blog and save a little time—and without always having to be the sole author:

1. **Invite guest blog contributors.** These can be friends, peers, or people you don't know. Put out a call for submissions and add submission guidelines to your site to attract content on a regular basis. As

an added bonus, guest contributors should also share a link to their work with their networks, bringing your site more traffic as a result.

2. **Compile round-up posts.** Ask a question and compile the responses into one long post—or a series of posts. You can conduct this effort via social media or submit your request via http://helpareporter.com.

3. **Share a link to an interesting article.** Blog posts don't always need to be long. You can post a quick paragraph with your thoughts on an article or industry news and include a link to the article so your readers can see it too. Remember, when you host a blog the goal should be to provide valuable information for your readers—whether that's information you create or it comes from other sources.

4. **Compile an index of previous posts.** If you've amassed a series of blog posts about a specific topic, put them all into one easy list for readers to discover. A friend of mine did this recently and reported a big boost in traffic as a result.

5. **Share a video.** Not all posts must be written. A quick video blog can attract new readers and give your carpal tunnel syndrome a break!

6. **Host a blog carnival.** A blog carnival is a round-up of links to other people's blog posts based on a theme. Some blogs feature these on a regular basis because they can be great for generating traffic. You can gather submissions and get more ideas via http://blogcarnival.com.

7. **Hold a comment contest.** Ask site visitors to post a comment with an answer to a trivia question or explaining how they do something. Give away a free ebook, audio recording series or other prize and enjoy the amount of buzz you can generate as a result.

8. **Compile industry news.** Become a valuable source for your readers by compiling a list of industry news stories. You might do this once each week or once a month. Whatever the interval, providing links to interesting industry information can be a great asset for your readers, and another way to build your brand as an authority in your field.

9. **Conduct interviews.** One of my favorite features that I added on BusinessInfoGuide.com is our column featuring interviews with entrepreneurs and authors. There is a simple contact form that users

can fill out and if the content is right for the site, we will feature the interview on the home page—and forever in our archives. This creates a win-win situation for all involved. The featured interviewee gets additional exposure from our site and social media, while we provide interesting content for our readers and ensure we're adding content to the site on a regular basis.

10. **Hire some help.** If the above suggestions still sound like a lot of work for you, then consider hiring someone to help. Hiring a blog content manager was one of the best decisions I've made. I still write all of my own content—and always will—but my content manager helps with round-ups, guest blog posts and other tasks that I no longer have to manage. This frees me up to focus on what I love to do and ensures that we consistently publish great content. A virtual assistant or an intern can make it all much easier in the long run. You can also hire a ghostwriter to help with content generation.

Write Better Blog Post Titles

In a world where we are all suffering from information overload, it is essential that blog titles catch the attention of prospective readers. A sizzling title inspires readers to click through and read more.

For example, if you came across the following blog titles on Facebook or Twitter, which would you be more likely to click?

10 Fun and Easy Halloween Costume Ideas for $20 or Less

Halloween Costume Ideas

For inspiration, take a close look at the covers of popular magazines. Magazine titles lead to sales, so they are carefully crafted to inspire readers. Here are some examples:

30 Ways to Lose 30 Pounds Before the Holidays

Plan a Dream Vacation on a Budget

Secrets to Looking 10 Years Younger Without Surgery

Following are strategies to help you write blog post titles that make readers want to read more:

Solutions – When you write blog posts that address the pain points of your target audience, you can capture the solutions in your titles. This is something the magazines do really well, as you can see from the examples above.

Lists – Online readers love quick and easy tips. Examples: *10 Ways to Earn More Money, 5 Solutions for Dry Winter Skin*, and 20 *Websites that Will Save You Money.*

Intrigue – Titles can hint at something that makes readers want to click. Examples: *Dog Training Secrets of Celebrity Trainers, 5 Things You Didn't Know About Your 401K*, or *Small Business Tax Saving Strategies You Might Be Missing.*

Controversy – Contrarian opinions and controversial positions grab attention. Take a stand against something in your industry or reveal details your audience doesn't know about. Example: *Money Down the Drain: Vitamins that You Probably Don't Need to Take.*

How To – Readers love prescriptive content, so starting a title with "How to" can easily grab attention. Examples: *How to Raise Happier Kids, How to Get More Mileage Out of Your Old Car*, or *How to Get More Exercise When You Don't Have Time to Spare.*

Humor – Readers love stories that make them laugh, so you can have some fun with your titles if humor is your thing. Example: *How to Get Your Own Gangnam Style.*

Titles can be challenging for all of us, myself included. Pay attention to which titles generate the most activity, and which ones fall flat, and do more of what works for your audience. Also, write great content. You can have fantastic titles, but your content also needs to meet expectations in order to build loyal readers who come back for more.

Email Marketing for Authors

The idea of managing email marketing for your book can sound like another obligation and time commitment, but it doesn't have to be that way. In fact, maintaining a mailing list requires very little time and more importantly, it can be *one of your best marketing tools.*

Permission to Market

When someone gives you their email address, they are giving you permission to market to them. This is powerful stuff that you shouldn't take lightly. Having mailing list subscribers is like having a golden ticket. These people want to be engaged with you and are inviting you to contact them.

Engagement

Sending out an email newsletter or other email marketing campaigns puts you in control of the communication with your audience. When you send out a new message, you have the attention of your subscribers—and you remind them about who you are and what you offer. Keeping them engaged over time helps build loyalty and leads to book sales, word-of-mouth marketing, online reviews, and other types of buzz generated as a result.

While social media is great for building your brand, and something I also advocate for authors, the big difference with email is that it puts you in the driver's seat. You can't control when someone chooses to view their social media accounts, but most people check email several times each day and you can greet them in their inbox.

Future Sales

You might have just one book now, but if you plan to write more in the future, or if you have other products or services to sell, then maintaining a mailing list is essential. When you can keep the attention of readers and convert them into loyal fans, they can continue to follow you for years. That means that they will also invest in your future offerings.

How to Get Started with Email Marketing

Get the right tool. If you use your regular email account and try to send an email out to 25 or more subscribers, your message probably won't make it through. Email servers have spam filters and sending out mass emails will trigger a halt on your message either from your outgoing mail server or from the recipients' mail servers. Because of this, you need a professional email tool. I use and recommend Constant Contact (http://constantcontact.com). It's easy to use, affordable, and offers all kinds of great features like contact management, sign-up box codes that you can place on your website, and a Facebook app so you can add a sign-up tab to your Facebook page.

Invite your friends and family. Once you choose a tool, invite your family and friends to sign up. You've got to start somewhere!

Offer a bonus for new subscribers. It's harder than ever to get people to give up their email address, so you have to make it worthwhile. Offer a bonus in exchange for signing up for your list, such as a sample chapter from your book or a special report.

Make it interesting. Your most important job is to make your e-newsletter interesting to recipients. Start with a brief personal greeting, which helps subscribers get to know you and feel a personal connection with you. Next, include an article of interest to your readers OR share the title and first paragraph of several recent blog posts and then include a link to continue reading each on your website. This is a great way to drive traffic back to your site while keeping readers engaged. You can also share resources, interesting facts and figures, upcoming appearances, links to media interviews, or event announcements. Don't forget to feature your book and mention another product or service if you have one.

Respect your list. It can be tempting to send a lot of email to your subscribers, but resist this inclination. If you inundate them, they may unsubscribe. Instead, limit your newsletter to once or twice each month. If something comes up in the meantime, you can always send out a quick special announcement.

Pay attention to stats. Your email marketing tool should provide you with data on open rates, the number of people who clicked a link in your message, and the number of unsubscribes. This is valuable information. Pay close attention to the data if you want to learn about the habits of your readers and what they like and don't like.

Build your list. In addition to having a sign-up box on your website, always look for ways to grow your mailing list. One of the best ways to do this is by collecting sign-ups when you speak at an event or host a book signing. Invite people to join—and don't forget to offer incentive. I often raffle off a book at the end of a presentation by collecting business cards from the audience. You can also promote your mailing list via your social media networks.

Act promptly. When you collect email addresses at an event, don't wait to acknowledge them. Get new subscribers added to your email system within a week and send out a welcome message that thanks them for attending your event.

Don't wait to get started. In 2005, I sent out my first newsletter to a grand total of eight subscribers. Today, it goes out to thousands of people. You have to start somewhere and find your groove. Your newsletter will likely evolve and change over time, and it should. Pay attention to what your subscribers like and don't like and give them more of what works. You may even go months or years without having anything to sell them and that is okay. When you're ready with your next book, you will have loyal subscribers who will be eager to support you.

Author Interview

Name: Patrick Schwerdtfeger

Website: http://www.bookpatrick.com

Books:

- *Marketing Shortcuts for the Self-Employed*
- *Webify Your Business*
- *Make Yourself Useful; Marketing in the 21ˢᵗ Century*

Are you traditionally published or self-published, and why did you make that choice?

I self-published my first two books (through Lulu.com) primarily because I didn't have a sufficient marketing platform to secure any traditional publishers. My second book, *Webify Your Business*, ended up doing fairly well so I was then able to secure a deal with John Wiley and Sons to essentially re-release an updated and expanded version of it, and that became my third book.

My primary income is as a speaker. I earn about 80% of my income from speaking fees. As a result, the third-party institutional credibility of being a Wiley author had plenty of benefits. The people who hire speakers work for either industry associations or large corporations, and in both cases, being a Wiley author gave me an edge over other potential speakers.

I have ambitions to write more books and will probably revert back to the self-publishing route. I am very grateful for the opportunity to work with

Wiley but also appreciate the increased control and profitability of modern self-publishing channels.

Tell us a bit about your most recent book:

Marketing Shortcuts for the Self-Employed is an updated and expanded version of *Webify Your Business*. The book has 80 chapters, each just three or four pages long, and they all end with an itemized to-do checklist. Originally, those chapters (or at least most of them) were emails in a free online course available on my website. Once subscribed, you would receive one 'marketing tip' each week via email for a full year. That's why the chapters are so short. Anything longer wouldn't have been practical in an email format.

I have read a lot of books in the 'small business marketing' niche and mine is, by far, the most tactical one. It's essentially an instruction manual. Each chapter covers a different strategy you can use to build credibility and gain exposure, and then offers specific steps you can take to begin taking action. People love those little checklists. Of all the feedback I've received, the checklists always come in first.

Who is your target audience of readers?

As the title suggests, the perfect reader is a self-employed service professional like a real estate agent, financial planner, insurance agent, yoga instructor, massage therapist, dentist, chiropractor or wedding planner, but it is also a great fit for small business owners and even larger organizations looking to employ some guerrilla-type marketing strategies. Last year I spoke at an eGovernment conference in Dubai and had my books available for sale. I have since heard that my book has been used by a government department in the United Arab Emirates attempting to raise awareness for their online service initiative within the local population.

What has been the single most effective marketing strategy you have used for promoting your book?

The most effective thing I have done to promote my book is my speaking career. During the past five years, I have spoken at over 350 events in North America, the Caribbean, Europe, the Middle East and Asia, resulting in a wide variety of benefits. I obviously sold a lot of books at those events but I also got a lot of high quality one-way inbound links to my website, raising its

Google PageRank, as well as bulk book sales to groups I never would've had access to otherwise.

Modern marketing is an indirect science. You always have an immediate target in mind but the largest benefits often come in through the side door. High quality links to your website make it rank higher for hundreds or even thousands of related keyword phrases. That's a massive benefit. Also, positive recommendations on Amazon go a long way to build credibility within that marketplace. While these examples don't translate directly into dollars, they both add momentum to the marketing process.

What are some other marketing tactics that have or haven't worked for you?

When I first released the book, I summarized it into 300 marketing tips and then released those as tweets on Twitter. They went out automatically, once each day for 300 days and then repeated from the beginning again. It was a good strategy, and each tip had a link back to the book's website. It generated a lot of curiosity and accounted for about 30% of my website traffic early on.

I used a service called ProfNet, offered by PRNewswire, to land some media exposure and that was quite successful as well. The service costs about $1,000 per year and connects experts with journalists looking for quotes. I received between 10 and 20 media inquiries per day and generated mentions in *CNN Money*, the *San Francisco Chronicle*, *The New York Times*, *Fortune Magazine*, Forbes.com and *MONEY Magazine* among many others.

The biggest failure was my outreach to the blogging community. Before the book was released, I reached out to about 700 bloggers and offered advance copies for their review. 130 replied and requested a copy. I did the campaign on my own dime and got less than a dozen reviews as a result. The problem was that I never developed real relationships with these bloggers. I believe the strategy has merit but you need to really connect with these people before they'll do anything to promote your work. In hindsight, it makes perfect sense. I just wish I would've thought about it more before spending my limited marketing budget ineffectively.

How has social media impacted your success? Which social media networks do you feel generate the best results for you?

As I mentioned above, Twitter was an effective vehicle for me. It gave me a quick and inexpensive way to spread the word. But overall, my success with social media was somewhat limited. It's interesting because I study social media case histories extensively and speak about that subject regularly, but it also takes a certain type of person to harness the power.

Women are generally better at social media than men. Men shout. I'm guilty of that myself. Men often publish content aggressively but don't engage with their audiences as much. By contrast, women interact. They do it well and that's what social media is all about. It's about interaction. It's about relationships. And not surprisingly, women are generally more effective at it than men. So I'm a huge proponent of social media but also encourage aspiring authors to focus on interaction and engagement as essential elements of any social media campaign.

What have been some of the biggest benefits of publishing a book?

If you have dreams of writing a book, write it now. Like, now! It will change your life. Arguably, people shouldn't treat you any differently when you've written a book, but they do. People treat you differently. And the funny thing is that no matter how many books you end up writing, you only 'become an author' once. You become an author when you publish your first book and it changes the way people look at you.

It's important to realize that most people never sell even 1,000 copies of their book. Most authors do very little with their book, and the eventual benefits you get from the undertaking are directly correlated to your efforts to leverage it. You need to get it out there. You need to sell it. You need to do some shameless self-promotion. But if you do, it can dramatically improve your life.

For me, the benefits revolve around credibility. It opens doors for me, attracts consulting clients, secures speaking engagements and allows me to introduce myself to just about anyone without worrying that I'm unworthy of their time. I'm an author. I have a book. So if I want to speak with someone important, I send them a copy along with a short note introducing myself. When I follow up with a phone call, they almost always give me some of their time.

What advice would you offer to new authors who are getting ready to promote their books?

New authors need to find ways to stay engaged with their readers. The weakness of printed books is that they come with no digital connection. Once a book has been purchased, the interaction often stops at that point. The best vehicle for staying in touch with readers is to maintain an active blog on the book's website.

From my own experience, I highly recommend authors include 'homework' in every blog post. The itemized to-do lists in my book have been the biggest reason for its success. People are looking for ways to put your knowledge to work in their own lives and an implementation checklist helps them do it. Every time you write a new blog post, think about the steps necessary to implement your advice, and include those steps at the bottom.

I also recommend authors include an email subscription option at the bottom of every blog post. "If you like this post, subscribe below and we'll notify you of future posts." If this is included on every post, you will be amazed at the exponential affect as your total number of posts increases. And by developing an active email list, you can drive a lot more traffic to your blog when you publish a new post.

If you were starting over today, is there anything you would do differently?

One of the biggest mistakes I made was to change my focus from one website to another. My first large-scale blog was called Tactical Execution but that name was long and clumsy. When I released "Marketing Shortcuts for the Self-Employed" in 2011, I started a new blog called 80shortcuts.com but that wasn't a great idea, either. Clearly, the rest of my life would be defined by more than just one book so I would eventually have to create something new.

The situation was complicated further by my long 13-letter German last name. That made my PatrickSchwerdtfeger.com website difficult to find. So finally, I registered BookPatrick.com and pointed that domain to PatrickSchwerdtfeger.com to make it easier. Will I change everything yet again? Who knows? I hope not but the lesson is clear. Find one primary domain that you're comfortable with and stick with it.

Is there anything else you would like to add?

Most people overestimate what they can accomplish in a year but dramatically underestimate what they can accomplish in a decade. Take a long-range approach to the project. There's a cumulative result that takes shape after a while. Everything you have done adds to everything else. A critical mass is reached where first-time visitors to your website are sufficiently impressed to take mental inventory of your work.

Have faith that your victories, however small, are cumulative. Success is the accumulation of 10,000 tiny victories and 100,000 tiny failures. It's all part of the process. Take risks. Try new things. Some will work. Others will fail. But over time, you will build a foundation of awareness and credibility with your audience and that's where the fun part begins!

Chapter 3:
Social Media Mastery

"Be yourself; everyone else is already taken."
– Oscar Wilde

I HATE TO BREAK IT TO YOU, but social media isn't going away. It will certainly evolve and change over time, but this method of communicating is here to stay. I believe it's one of the most powerful ways for authors to build an audience and to connect with that audience. You can learn a lot about what's on the mind of your readers by paying attention to their feedback, comments, and questions online.

Twitter Success

Of all the social media networks, Twitter is my favorite. As an author, it allows me to locate and connect with my audience. It's also been a fantastic force for driving traffic to my website, generating sales, and attracting media interviews. If you're an author and you still aren't sure if Twitter is right for you, following are some reasons to reconsider:

1. **Cultivate Your Fan Base** – One of the many reasons why Twitter users love this platform is that it is easy to connect with authors, news sites, and celebrities. Current and future readers are spending time on Twitter and they are seeking interesting people to follow. You should be one of them!

2. **Instant Feedback** – The real-time, fast-paced action on Twitter is part of its major appeal. You can ask a question and get immediate responses. Your readers can share their thoughts with you. Twitter can be downright addictive once you understand its power, and can

be useful in helping you understand what is on the minds of your readers.

3. **Media Opportunities** – Media professionals, including reporters, editors, and producers, are using Twitter on a daily basis. More importantly, they are searching Twitter to find sources for stories. If you maintain an active Twitter account, you increase the likelihood of being found.

4. **Twitter Stats Are Climbing** - According to a report from <u>Compete.com</u>, Twitter is currently one of the top 20 websites in the world. User engagement is also up on Twitter, with visitors spending an average of over 9 minutes on the site with each visit. Further <u>research by Compete</u> shows that 56% of users who follow a brand on Twitter say they are more likely to make a purchase from that brand, while only 47% of Facebook users said the same for brand "Likes."

5. **Increase Website Traffic** – Each time you publish a new post on your blog, share it with your Twitter audience (title plus the link to read the full post). Twitter is a tremendous source for driving website traffic.

6. **Get Extra Mileage from Blog Content** – As you share each new blog post, you should also schedule it to repeat. We aren't all looking at Twitter at the same time, and because content updates happen frequently, you are likely missing the bulk of your audience if you only tweet a blog post one time. I recommend tweeting each new post once on the first day, again the next day, again a week later, and then every other week for 90 days (stagger the days and times). Twitter users don't care when the content was written, as long as it is still relevant. This strategy will increase engagement and traffic to your site. You can download a free Twitter tracking schedule here: <u>http://nonfictionauthorsassociation.com/book-downloads/</u>.

7. **Build Your Following** – One important way to increase your followers on Twitter is by making an effort to follow other people. You can't just sit back and wait for people to find you. Instead, look for them. Search for Twitter users by keywords related to your book topic. Also, search for media professionals who cover your topic. A great source for finding media pros on Twitter is <u>MuckRack.com</u>.

The hope is that the people you follow will check you out and follow you back.

8. **Generate Sales** – When you cultivate an audience on Twitter by sharing great content, you build loyal fans. Then, when you have something to sell—like a new book release or a companion product or service—you will have a captive audience interested in buying what you have to offer.

9. **Get Found** – As you share content on Twitter, you should start to notice new followers. Many will find you based on the keywords in your tweets. For example, if you tweet vegan recipes, Twitter users who are searching for "vegan" and "vegan recipes" will find you and likely follow you as a result. Some will even retweet your post to their followers.

10. **Share Content from Other Sources** – Follow industry news sources and experts who share content your audience would enjoy, and then retweet their content to your audience. The point is to become a resource for your audience and give value, even if the content isn't always yours. This can also help you gain favor and recognition from those whose content you share.

11. **Have a Human Presence** – Engage with your audience by thanking them for retweets, answering questions, and asking questions. Don't automate everything. Instead, show them that you're paying attention.

12. **Track Keywords** – You can monitor keywords on Twitter to see tweets by users covering your designated word or phrase, and then you can reach out to them. For example, if you've authored a book on how to travel through Italy, you could monitor keyword mentions for "Italy," "Italian vacation," etc. Then, when you find related posts, send a tweet to the user saying, "*@bizauthor – Heading to Italy? Bet you'd love the Guide to Your Best Vacation in Italy! <link>."* Yes, this may sound corny and it will take time to execute, but it can be effective. Use http://tweetscan.com to find current tweets by keyword.

13. **Share Photos** – Twitter isn't just about text. Share photos (like your book cover!) using http://twitpic.com.

14. **Share Videos** – If you record videos, easily share them with http://twitvid.com.

15. **Follow Back** – I believe in following back users who follow me. It's a good way to repay the social currency of a new follower, and if you want your readers/customers to know you're paying attention, it just makes sense to follow them back. You can automate the follow back process with a subscription from http://socialoomph.com.

16. **Send Direct Messages** – When new users follow you on Twitter, you can send a direct message with a note of thanks. Leverage SocialOomph to set up an automatic direct message. I use mine to invite users to my Facebook page (with link). You could also invite them to your website, your book's listing on Amazon, etc.

17. **Conduct a Poll/Survey** – Get user engagement by posting compelling poll topics and then sharing results. Try http://pollyourfollowers.com or create a survey with http://surveymonkey.com and tweet it out.

18. **Make it Easy to Monitor** – Tweetdeck (http://tweetdeck.com) is a free tool that you can use to monitor Twitter activity. When your audience grows, this tool will help keep it manageable. You can also easily retweet and respond to posts with Tweetdeck. I recommend creating columns to monitor mentions of your Twitter handle, those you've added to a list of Favorites, and search columns for your book title and website links.

19. **Pay with a Tweet** – Here's a nifty app that you can use for book promotion or other giveaways. Pay With a Tweet (http://paywithatweet.com) is a free service where you can create a button for your site and allow visitors to download a freebie (ebook, sample chapters, special report, etc.) in exchange for a tweet. This is a fun way to build some buzz and engage new readers.

20. **Cross-Promote** – Your social networks shouldn't stand alone. Cross-promote your Twitter account on Facebook, LinkedIn, and Google+. Periodically invite your followers on other social media platforms to come on over to Twitter, and vice versa.

21. **Customize** – Have a graphic designer create a custom Twitter background and header image.

22. **Use Hashtags** – A hashtag is a keyword with a pound sign in front of it, and looks like this: #marketing. Hashtags are used on Twitter to help users search for content. For example, during the 2012 election, President Obama's team promoted the hashtag #Forward. When a follower tweeted something related to the campaign and included that hashtag, it made it easier for other participants to see. While you don't need to stuff your content full of hashtags, they can be used occasionally to indicate the subject matter of your post. For example, you might tweet a new blog post that looks like this: *How to Grow Prize Winning Roses <link> #gardening #roses.*

23. **Host a Twitter Chat** - Conduct an interview with an industry expert or simply with your Twitter audience by hosting a Twitter chat event. This is something you can host one time, or on an ongoing basis. Melinda Emerson, who is known as the Small Biz Lady on Twitter, has over 100k Twitter followers thanks to her weekly Small Biz Chat events. Assign a hashtag to your event, such as #moneychat, and invite your users to join in. Use a tool like Tweet Grid (http://tweet-grid.com) to make it easier to manage.

24. **Get Listed in Directories** - Improve your chances of being discovered on Twitter by listing your Twitter handle (user name) with directories: http://wefollow.com, http://twiends.com, http://twellow.com, http://justtweetit.com, and http://tweetfind.com.

25. **Find the Fun** – If managing your social media presence feels like an obligation, it will probably never get the results you want. It works best when you have fun and truly enjoy it. I have to say that I'm a Twitter addict. I use it as a learning tool and to stay on top of industry trends. It's also rewarding to hear from readers, watch your content get retweeted, and realize that you're making an impact on people's lives.

Commit to making it something fun you do each day and you will be rewarded with greater results. Also, it doesn't have to be a huge time commitment. I spend less than 30 minutes per day on social media since I pre-schedule most of my content and peek in on Twitter in between calls and activities. Once you find your groove, it gets a lot easier and you'll realize that it can be a worthwhile investment of your time. If you absolutely don't have time to manage social media, we offer affordable management services at Authority Publishing: http://authoritypublishing.com/marketing/social-media-marketing-services/.

Facebook Fans

One of the biggest benefits that social media platforms like Facebook provide is the ability to get repeat exposure with the people in your network. Readers, peers, and prospects can make up your network, and you can promote author events, sales, special offers and more through your Facebook page. Unfortunately, Facebook has made it increasingly difficult for business users to gain exposure without paying for advertising. You might have 1,000 page fans, but only 10% to 20% of them will actually see your updates in their news feeds. This can be extremely frustrating and may drive business users away from Facebook as better options surface, but for now we must live with it.

I still believe it's worthwhile to maintain a presence on Facebook if there is a chance your readers are spending time there. And unless you've authored a book on nuclear physics, there's a good chance at least some of your target audience is hanging out on Facebook.

Here are some ways to maximize Facebook for book marketing:

Create a Powerful Business Page – Facebook doesn't want users to promote their businesses with personal profiles, so it's important that you create a business page. The most important decision you will have when creating your page is what name to use. You can create a page for your book, but if you plan to write future books, you'll be stuck managing multiple pages. I recommend building a page for you personally, as an author branding tool.

Make sure you fill out your profile with as much detail as possible, and include a professional author photo. Also have a graphic designer create a custom banner image for you.

Communicate with Wall Posts – Your page features a "wall" where you can share updates with your audience. Share all of your new blog posts here by simply posting the title and link. Facebook will automatically generate a preview. You can also share videos, photos, inspirational quotes (though these are highly overused), quick tips, questions, surveys, event announcements, and anything else you can think of to engage your audience. Posting one to three times per day is plenty on Facebook.

Interact with Your Audience – Whenever someone comments on one of your posts on Facebook, take time to acknowledge them with a quick note of thanks. Answer questions and generally demonstrate for your audience that you are paying attention.

Remove Junk – Spammers exist everywhere online. Delete spammy comments that show up on your page.

Pin to Top – When you hover over the upper right corner of a post on your Facebook page and click the edit icon, there is a "Pin to Top" option. When you select this, it moves that post to the top of your page and keeps it there until you unpin it. Any subsequent posts that you add to your page will appear below your pinned post. This can be really handy if you want to promote something that is time-sensitive such as a current promotion that you're holding or an upcoming event.

Highlight – When you hover over the upper right corner of a post on your Facebook page, you'll see a star icon called "Highlight." Selecting this option will expand your post from a small box to a feature that spans across both columns. This is a nice way to draw attention to a specific post on your page. You can also highlight multiple posts and they will remain that way until you click the icon again to remove highlight. The highlight feature is also available for use on your personal Facebook profile.

Promote Your Posts – You can pay Facebook to ensure a specific post on your wall gets exposure with your audience and beyond. You can set a budget of as little as $5 to promote a post. This can be quite useful when you want to raise awareness for a recent post, especially if you are promoting something such as a book launch or upcoming event.

Paid Advertising – Facebook offers two types of advertising: pay-per-click and pay-per-view. The pay-per-click option can be an effective way to add new followers to your page. You can specify demographics by keywords and location, and Facebook will serve up your ads to people who meet that criteria. Advertising on Facebook is not cheap. You will set a bid price for clicks, which Facebook will suggest at $1 per click and up. However, you can also set your bid at a lower rate of $.65 to $.85 per click and your ads will still run, though probably not as often as they would with a higher rate. But with a budget of just $5 per day, or about $150 per month, you can steadily build your audience. And even though you'll be paying for each click, your ad will still get thousands of impressions (views) for each click generated, so that visibility alone can help to build your brand.

 Social media time management is a big complaint for authors. One way to manage it all is by pre-scheduling your status updates. I use and recommend http://hootsuite.com for scheduling posts to Facebook, Twitter, LinkedIn, and Google+. If you write and schedule blog posts in advance (and you should because this saves time, too!), you can then schedule your social media posts ahead of time, too.

Link Your Personal Facebook Profile with Your Business Page

If you have a personal Facebook profile, be sure to link it to your business page so that your Facebook friends can easily connect with you there, too. On your personal Facebook profile, just under your photo, is the area where you list where you work—and your employer can be a link to your business page. Here's how:

1. From your personal profile, click on the box below your photo that lists where you work.

2. Click on "Edit" in the Work and Education section.

3. Start typing in the title of your business page. Facebook should reveal a drop-down menu where you can click to select your page.

4. Fill in your title, location, and description. Be sure to click "Save Changes."

That's it—you're done!

How to Convert Your Personal Facebook Profile into a Business Page

One of the lesser known features offered by Facebook is the ability to convert your personal profile into a business page. Because Facebook has strict policies requiring personal profiles be used by people, not businesses, it has offered up an easy way to make the transition.

Turning your profile into a page has some additional benefits and considerations. Business pages on Facebook are searchable by Google, which can be beneficial for business. Your friends will also get transferred over and listed as page "Likes," so if you have a lot of friends, your page will be off to a good start!

When you convert your profile into a page, you will lose all of your data so Facebook recommends that you download a copy of your Timeline for future reference. Here's how:

1. Go to "Account Settings" from the drop-down menu in the upper right.

2. Click on "Download a Copy of Your Facebook Data." The data downloaded will include details of your timeline, a list of friends, photos and videos you've uploaded to your page, and more.

Once you convert to a business page, you will need to start over by updating your timeline and adding details to the page. You might also want to post an announcement on your page to alert your friends about the transition.

Convert your personal Facebook profile into a business page here: https://www.facebook.com/pages/create.php?migrate.

AUTHOR TIP: If you aren't yet working with a graphic designer and want to have custom social media headers designed, consider hiring someone from http://fiverr.com. This site is loaded with contractors who will do work for just $5, and you can get some dazzling social media images created here.

Promote with Pinterest

According to a 2012 report by Experian.com, Pinterest is the third largest social media site based on the number of site visits each month. To put the numbers in perspective, Facebook stood out above the rest with a whopping 7 billion visits, Twitter received 182 million, Pinterest received 104 million, and LinkedIn received 86 million. Considering Pinterest has only been in existence since 2010, its growth has been remarkable.

Pinterest is a social media site built around the concept of sharing photos and videos. Pinterest users can "pin" photos or videos to their "boards" for sharing with other users. With a predominantly female audience, Pinterest is a popular place to share images for wedding planning, home redecorating, recipes, vacation destinations, and books. But your book doesn't need to fall into these categories to take advantage of the power of Pinterest.

In fact, like all of the other social media networks, Pinterest can potentially drive a lot of traffic to your website. I recently went to Google to search for the title of a blog post I wrote awhile back. I was surprised to see that the first result on Google wasn't from my blog, it was from the pinned photo of that blog post on Pinterest! This site can be powerful and a lot of fun.

Here's how to get started with Pinterest:

Create pin boards. When defining your boards, consider what topics and images would be of interest to your target audience. You can create multiple boards with various themes and should avoid using the default board titles that Pinterest suggests. Instead, rename your boards with descriptive, keyword-rich titles to help Pinterest users find your content. Google also gives a high priority to boards on Pinterest, so that keyword-rich title has a good chance of showing up in search results.

Download the Pin It button. Pinterest allows you to download a Pin It button to add to the toolbar on your web browser. This makes it easy to get in the habit of pinning interesting content to your boards.

Start pinning content. One of the great benefits of pinning photos to Pinterest is that a link is automatically included back to the source of the pinned photo. So if you pin a book from Amazon, the image will be linked back to the book's page on Amazon. You can also add descriptions to each photo that you pin to your board so be sure to include a descriptive title. Here are some examples of content you can pin to your boards:

- Books in the same genre as yours, including your books of course. For example, you could create a board called "Favorite European Travel Books." Since Pinterest automatically links back to the source of the photo, be sure to pin your books either from a sales page on your site or a sales page on one of the online retailers. For extra assurance that visitors will click through to buy your book, you can also copy and paste the sales page link into the description for the image.

- Blog content from your own blog. For each new blog post, pin its associated photo to a board you have designated for your blog. Pinterest will automatically link back to the source of the photo so that visitors can easily click through to read your content. For example, you might create a board called "ABC Travel Blog – How to Travel Through Europe."

- Photos from events including book signings, speaking engagements, launch parties, etc.

- Themes from your book. If your book is set in a specific city, you could pin photos of various city monuments. If your book includes recipes or food-related topics, pin photos of food with links back to the recipes online. Look for interesting ways to promote visual elements from your books.

- Photos from readers. Ask readers to submit photos of themselves reading your books and have some fun pinning these to a board. If your book has a pet-related theme, you could ask readers to take pictures of your book with their dogs and cats! Or ask readers to send photos of your book from their vacation destinations. Have some fun with this and get others engaged in the process.

- Unrelated content also works on Pinterest. I recently created a board called "Creative Wall Art Ideas," and began pinning photos I found through searching Google and Pinterest. That board has generated a lot of re-pins from Pinterest users, which increases my overall engagement on Pinterest. We don't know Pinteret's algorithms for ranking users, but it most likely assigns higher priority to users with active boards.

Build your audience. You can cross-promote your Pinterest presence with other social networks by periodically sharing links to your boards on Facebook, Twitter, etc. Also, be sure to add a link to your Pinterest profile from your website alongside your other social media site links.

Engage on Pinterest. Spend some time visiting Pinterest boards created by other users where you can choose to follow a user, leave a comment on a photo, like their photo, or re-pin their photo to one of your boards. As with all of the other social networks, the more you participate, the better results you will see as other Pinterest users begin to return the favor.

Add a Pin It button to your site. To encourage website visitors to share your content on Pinterest, install a Pin It button across all pages and blog posts on your website. WordPress users can easily install the Pinterest Pin It button plug-in or add the button from the ShareThis social media plug-in (search plug-ins in WordPress to locate these).

Get creative with your pins. Start paying attention to the content you come across online and pin interesting articles, news, info graphics, short stories, poems, or products to a board on your site (you can always create a new board if needed). As long as the content appeals to your target audience, anything goes. You might be surprised to discover how many others will begin to engage with you, visit your website, and repin your content as a result.

LinkedIn Leads

For any author in the business arena, LinkedIn is an important place to maintain a social media presence. Though it's substantially smaller than Facebook, the audience on LinkedIn consists primarily of business professionals. Here are some ways to leverage LinkedIn:

Create a Content-Rich Profile – LinkedIn gives its users a lot of space to add content to a profile, and you should take advantage of all of it. Fill out a thorough job history, and feature your current author endeavors under your most current employment. Add links to your website and other social media profiles, and upload a professional head shot.

Import Your Contacts – You can export your contacts from your email system, and easily import them into LinkedIn. And don't worry about spamming your contacts. LinkedIn will display them in a list and show you who is already using LinkedIn so that you can send connection requests only to those who already have a presence there.

Update Your Activity – Similar to your Facebook wall, you can share announcements on LinkedIn. Start by sharing each new blog post (title and link). Though LinkedIn users aren't as active with reading news updates from their networks as people are on Facebook, many users subscribe to a daily email with network updates, and your new posts will show up there. This is great for building brand recognition.

Request Recommendations – You can reach out to people within your LinkedIn network to request recommendations, which will appear on your profile. This is a fantastic way to get reviews for your books, as well as for speaking engagements and your work. You can also give recommendations for others, which can in turn lead them to give you a recommendation.

Use Advanced Search – This is one of my favorite features on LinkedIn. With advanced search, you can locate people based on keywords. For example, if you want to reach the person in charge of the Back-to-School contest at Staples, you could search by company name of Staples and keyword "Back to School." It's amazing how much information is available on LinkedIn profiles. This can be useful if you're pursuing bulk sales with companies and need to find the right contact, or if you want to pitch the person who is in charge of running a particular industry event. LinkedIn won't let you email people you aren't directly connected to; however, for a nominal fee, you can become a LinkedIn advanced user and will be granted a certain number of LinkedIn mail messages per month.

Participate in Groups – One of the best places to interact on LinkedIn is within its very active groups. Here you can find all kinds of professional groups, some with just a few hundred members, and some with tens of thousands. This is such an important feature on LinkedIn that I have expanded on it below.

How to Market Yourself on LinkedIn Groups Without Annoying People

I run the Nonfiction Authors Network on LinkedIn and as the group has grown to nearly 3,000 members, moderating the message board has become more challenging. The biggest time-waster comes from the people who spam the group with unwanted messages by posting links to their blogs where the content isn't related to writing or publishing, and blatant promotional announcements and stuff that is just downright inappropriate.

What people don't seem to realize is that they aren't making friends by violating group policies. They are instead alienating themselves from fellow members. While other forum owners take a more laid back approach and allow spam to clog up their networks, I quickly ban repeat offenders.

Despite the challenges, I still believe that participating in forums can be a great way to establish yourself as an authority in your field and to attract book readers. Here are some simple guidelines to make the most out of LinkedIn groups.

Choose Your Groups – While you can join many groups on LinkedIn, it's not realistic to think you can participate regularly with all of them. Choose one or two where your target audience can be found and make a point of being active there. LinkedIn displays the most active forum participants along the right sidebar so consistent effort can pay off with extra recognition.

Review Guidelines – Most groups have clear member guidelines and rules. Be sure to review these so you understand what the boundaries are.

Answer Questions – If you want to position yourself as an authority, demonstrate your knowledge by contributing to forum conversations. Provide value and members will notice.

Promote in Context – Mention your services carefully and in proper context. If a member asks for tips when redesigning a website and you are a web designer, this is an opportunity to respond with: "As a web designer, here are my suggestions…" or "In my book, XYZ, I talk about this at greater length."

Ask Questions – Engage with the group by soliciting feedback from fellow members.

Share Blog Posts – If appropriate and within group guidelines, share your latest blog posts if they relate to the topic of the forum, but don't just be a drive-by poster. If you're going to share your blog, also make sure to actively engage in other conversations. As a group owner and user, I find it obnoxious when members do nothing but blog-bomb the group message board.

Respond to Comments – Pay attention to responses to message threads where you are involved and acknowledge those who reach out to you.

Show Personality – You can really stand out on a forum by being witty, thoughtful, and smart.

When in Doubt, Ask – The forum moderator will appreciate you checking in to ask about what is appropriate. This is also an opportunity to get to know the group leader and perhaps offer to help out. Co-moderators can also gain added visibility on the site and based on my own experience, most moderators would welcome offers of additional support.

Subscribe to Updates – LinkedIn allows you to subscribe to an email summary for each group that you belong to, which will show up in your inbox daily and allow you to see the latest activity on the group's board. This is a handy way to scan group activity without having to login to LinkedIn so that you can decide if there is something you want to respond to.

Join the Nonfiction Authors Network on LinkedIn—it's free! http://www.linkedin.com/groups/Nonfiction-Authors-Network-2950959

How to Start and Grow a LinkedIn Group

1. **Choose a Niche Topic** – Before you start a group, search through existing groups to make sure you have a unique idea. If similar groups already exist, see what they are lacking. If the groups are small, then your opportunity is probably greater than if they are large. Better yet, narrow the niche for your group. I found several writers' groups on LinkedIn, but none specifically for nonfiction authors. It was an opportunity and I grabbed the chance to lead a niche group. You'll have an easier chance of success if your focus is on a largely untapped niche and meet a need for your target audience.

2. **Create Your Group** – Give your group a clear and compelling title. Have a logo created. Write policies for how you want members to engage in your group. Take it seriously and set it up for success.

3. **Send Invitations** – LinkedIn makes it easy to invite your contacts to participate in the group and you should do so immediately. Give your friends and peers a nudge and ask them to help you get the activity moving.

4. **Ask Members to Introduce Themselves** – Your first post should be an invitation for introductions. This is an ideal ice breaker to get the conversations started.

5. **Ask Additional Questions** – You might ask members to share their social media links, comment on an industry trend or news, or share their experiences. Log in daily to post questions until you start getting activity from members. It shouldn't take long to increase activity if your membership is growing and soon conversations will start naturally among members.

6. **Share Relevant Information** – If you come across an interesting news story or article, share it with your group.

7. **Lead By Example** – Ask compelling questions, answer member questions, and engage with humor and style. When you show others how it's done, it will be easier for them to emulate.

8. **Cross-Promote** – Make sure to let all of your networks know about your group. Share a link to the group via your other social media outlets, on your website, in your newsletter, email signature, etc. Promotion should be an ongoing effort.

9. **Ask Members to Invite Friends** – Sometimes all you have to do is ask!

10. **Keep the Momentum Going** – If things slow down or are slow to start, ask friends and peers to help by sharing their questions and resources. Sometimes just two or three people can make a big difference.

11. **Check in Often** – Managing your group doesn't need to be a major time-consuming undertaking, though you should have a daily presence there as much as possible. Deal with spammer issues immediately (some members will share nothing but promotional posts—warn them and delete them). Some members will require moderation and others will need to be reminded of the rules. Occasionally post a reminder about guidelines. Members will appreciate that you care enough to moderate the group and ensure it's a productive place for all.

12. **Appoint Co-Moderators** – If managing the group is too much for you or you simply don't want to go it alone, ask members or peers if they would like to be co-moderators. This can lighten your workload and breed goodwill.

Don't forget to have fun! Your attitude about your group will come across, so make sure it's something you enjoy doing. Your members will notice and membership will grow as a result.

Get Google+

Of the top five social media networks, Google+ is my least favorite. However, because it's owned by Google it does matter and you should leverage it to build your audience and promote your content. Here's how:

Create a Page – Similar to Facebook, Google wants its users to use business pages instead of personal profiles for business purposes. You can get started here: https://plus.google.com/pages/create.

Complete Profile Details – Make sure to click on the "Edit" button to update your bio and contact information. You can also upload a profile photo, which can be a photo of you or your book (remember, I prefer to brand the author, but it's your choice). You can also import a custom profile header image.

Update Settings – There are a couple of dozen notification settings in Google+ and you'll want to turn most of them off. I find it helpful to get notified when someone tags me or comments on one of my posts. This prevents me from having to login to Google+ to check very often. The rest can be disabled.

Grow Your Circles – Circles are Google's version of page Likes. You can add people to your circles and when you do, their updates will show up in your news feed. However, Google won't let you start adding people to your circles until someone adds your page to theirs. Ask a friend to do you the favor of adding you to their circles to get the ball rolling.

Share Updates – As with the other social media networks, start by sharing your recent blog posts. Ask questions, share surveys, and engage your audience. Respond to comments and generally engage when possible.

Participate in Hangouts and Communities – Hangouts are private chat groups conducted on Google, and communities are similar to Groups on LinkedIn. Consider both optional, but if you want to dig in, lots of options await.

Pursue +1s – One of the biggest benefits of Google+ is the +1 feature that is displayed next to all posts. When someone clicks +1 for your latest blog post, Google pays attention. More importantly, Google pays attention when that post gets a lot of activity. So if you can generate a lot of interest for a blog post with Google+, it's quite likely Google will give that post priority ranking in its search engine.

AUTHOR TIP:

Google has a program known as authorship, which will display your name (byline) and photo in Google search results next to content that you write. This can be great for brand recognition! It's relatively easy to set up authorship, and since it's likely the steps will change, here's a link to find Google's process: https://plus.google.com/authorship.

YouTube Video Marketing

There are plenty of benefits to marketing with video. YouTube is currently the second most searched website next to Google, and because it's owned by Google, YouTube videos receive top priority in the search engine. When you search for something on Google, like how to bake a cherry pie, inevitably at least one of the top ten search results will include a YouTube video with those same keywords.

Videos can be very powerful for generating traffic, especially when you incorporate keyword-rich titles. How-to videos can perform well on Google because people are searching for that kind of content, and many prefer to view videos over reading posts on the same topic.

Videos can be a great option for people who don't love to write, and for those who have natural charisma on camera. From talking head videos where you give some advice, to tutorials and demonstrations, videos can be another great way to get visibility with your audience and help them get to know you. Here are some tips for building a following on YouTube:

Keep Videos Short – For best results, limit most of your videos to two to five minutes. Short videos do well on YouTube due to short attention spans.

Create Your Own Channel – When you login to YouTube (using your Google login), you can create your own channel. It's free and easy to do. You can also fill out a profile with your bio and website link, and upload a custom background for your channel page.

Record Your Own Videos – The best news of all is that you don't need to spend big bucks on video production. In fact, YouTube users tend to favor videos that have a more homemade feel. A simple flip camera or even your phone can do the job, though it would be wise to invest in a good microphone for better sound quality. And be sure to have great lighting as well.

Get Editing – You can either learn how to edit your own videos or hire someone to help with this task. You may want to include an introductory image with your website link, or have a banner added across the bottom of your video that features your website link (similar to how your evening news show reveals a banner at the bottom of the screen). You can hire a video editor via elance.com or fiverr.com, or invest in editing software. YouTube also offers a free editing program: http://www.youtube.com/editor.

Post to Your Blog – Be sure to post new videos to your blog or a designated area of your website. YouTube provides HTML code for embedding videos, which will include a video player so site visitors can easily view your videos. This can be a great way to supplement written blog content.

Promote Via Social Media – Share your new video posts across all of your social networks.

Promote Beyond YouTube – Another great site for posting your videos is http://vimeo.com. One subscription-based service that you may also want to use is Traffic Geyser (http://trafficgeyser.com), which will post your videos across many online platforms for greater visibility.

Author Interview

Name: Bob Baker

Website: www.Bob-Baker.com, www.TheBuzzFactor.com, www.FullTimeAuthor.com

Books:

- *Guerrilla Music Marketing Handbook*
- *Guerrilla Music Marketing Online*
- *Guerrilla Music Marketing, Encore Edition*
- *55 Ways to Promote & Sell Your Book on the Internet*
- *Unleash the Artist Within*

Are you traditionally published or self-published, and why did you make that choice?

Of the eight physical books of mine that have been published over the past 20 years, six were self-published and two were traditionally published by smaller companies that have since gone out of business. My most successful and profitable books are the ones I put out myself independently.

I've always been stubbornly independent, so I embraced the DIY "life design" path long before it was hip to do so. Admittedly, my first book was traditionally published in 1992. It got me into the game and convinced me to dedicate my life to being an author, teacher and speaker. But I quickly explored the indie route in the mid-1990s and published everything from stapled special reports to audio cassettes (remember those?).

The first version of my bestselling title, called *Guerrilla Music Marketing Handbook*, came out in about 1995 in a three-ring binder. Within a few years, as digital and short-run printing developed, I turned it into a paperback version and continued to upgrade the packaging and design every couple of years.

Even though I wasn't published by an established, respected music business book publisher, I created one of the first resources that addressed the needs of the growing independent music movement. As a result, my reputation and exposure level grew. The book even made a cameo appearance in the major motion picture *The School of Rock*, starring Jack Black. I've been interviewed on NPR's "Morning Edition" and have enjoyed a lot of media exposure on my core topic of music marketing for independent artists.

I didn't listen to the standard advice that I "needed" a publisher to be taken seriously. Instead, I stayed focused on delivering value to my core audience: working musicians with a DIY mindset. And it has paid off. I've been a full-time author since 2004.

Tell us a bit about your most recent book:

My latest release is actually the most recent update to the *Guerrilla Music Marketing Handbook*. I spent many months completely revising and updating the chapters, especially the section on Internet music marketing.

Who is your target audience of readers?

Musicians, obviously. But not every musician. My ideal reader and fan is a musician (or a promoter or music publicist) who values education and is willing to get their hands dirty learning how to promote themselves (or their clients) better. They are either confused and overwhelmed by marketing and are seeking some easy, low-cost ways to promote their music, OR they already have a handle on marketing and simply want to learn more and do a better job at it.

So my target audience is a specific subset of all musicians. And this is something all authors should keep in mind as they write and promote their books. Even if you serve a niche group of readers, you can most likely break down how you define them even further. Doing so will make it easier to find them, speak to them, and cater to their unique worldview and needs.

What has been the single most effective marketing strategy you have used for promoting your books?

This one is easy. It was my #1 priority back in 1995, and it continues to be the most powerful marketing asset any author can have. I'm talking about an email list of readers and fans. If you are not actively building a mailing list, and then regularly communicating with your subscribers at least once a month, you are shooting yourself in the foot.

All other forms of marketing are passive: your website, media coverage, speaking events, a Facebook page, etc. People might notice them, but you have to rely on people to remember you and return to seek you out. But once someone has given you their name and email address (along with permission to follow up with them), you are in control and can dictate how often they hear from you and what messages you send. This is a powerful position to be in. So don't put off starting a mailing list. Do it today!

What are some other marketing tactics that have or haven't worked for you?

In addition to a mailing list, what's been most effective for me is sharing little chunks of my advice in the many places where my ideal readers congregate online.

When I first got online in the '90s, that sharing was mostly text-based – so I used articles on websites, email, discussion forums, and other avenues to share my words. In the early 2000's blogging began to take hold, so I used that new text-based tool to spread my message via my www.MusicPromotionBlog.com site, which houses more than 600 separate blog posts.

By 2004, podcasting became the new audio-based way for average people to create their own online radio shows, so I started the "Artist Empowerment Radio" podcast and later the "Internet Book Promotion" podcast.

In 2006, I started a YouTube channel and began posting short video clips sharing my marketing advice for musicians, writers, and more. I have close to 100 videos on my channel as of this writing.

These days this multimedia approach is called "content marketing." For me, it's always been about spreading small, bite-sized chunks of my advice through whatever means would help me reach my ideal readers most effectively. Doing this increases my name recognition, inspires more people to get on my mailing list, and ultimately helps me sell more books.

How has social media impacted your success? Which social media networks do you feel generate the best results for you?

Social media is a wonderful thing, but sadly there's no single best site for all authors. It's up to each author to determine which network will serve them best. Like most things in life, you get out of it what you put in. For me, I spend the bulk of my time on Facebook, Twitter and YouTube – while also posting regularly to my blogs, podcasts, and email newsletters.

What have been some of the biggest benefits of publishing a book?

To me, a book is simply one expression of a bigger mission that you have in life. Ideally, you have a story you feel needs to be told, or a message you need to get out, or valuable lessons you've learned that you feel compelled to share. A book is one great way to reach more people with your message – along with public speaking, blogging, media coverage, and more.

So personal satisfaction is a big benefit, especially when it's tied to a bigger mission of helping, educating, or inspiring others.

Having one or more books out also boosts your credibility, which you can leverage into a small business if you prefer. Once you gain a readership (and a mailing list), you can take the content of your book and turn it into a workshop, online course, one-on-one consulting, and more.

What advice would you offer to new authors who are getting ready to promote their books?

It's never too early to start building a readership, even long before you have a book out. Also, think of your first book as laying the foundation for future growth. Think big, but don't set yourself up to be crushed when sales are slower than you had hoped. Think long term and what your overall mission and message are.

If you were starting over today, is there anything you would do differently?

Not really. Building an email list and relentless content marketing are the two things I would still focus on.

PART
TWO:

Book Launch

Chapter 4:
Build Your Launch Plans

"Twenty years from now you will be more disappointed by the things that you didn't do than by the ones you did do. So throw off the bowlines. Sail away from the safe harbor. Catch the trade winds in your sails. Explore. Dream. Discover."
— H. Jackson Brown Jr.

PLANNING FOR THE LAUNCH of your book can be loaded with emotion. All at once it is exciting, overwhelming, and fraught with nerves. For a lot of authors, it also stirs up a feeling of vulnerability. Propelling your book into the world for all to see can feel like a risky move, opening you up for criticism. But I've never had an author tell me she regretted achieving the goal of authoring a book.

Here's the reality: There will be critics. There is no way around that. And that's true for just about anything that's worth doing in life. Don't let that stop you or slow you down. Instead, push through the fear and have fun with the launch. Yes, you will probably get a negative review somewhere down the road. So what? All authors do. Some of those reviews can provide good feedback for your future books, and some will just come from unhappy people who have nothing better to do than dish out cranky reviews. That's their problem, not yours. The vast majority of people will offer you praises and enjoy your work, so let that be your guide.

Product Launch Promotion Checklist

A lot of effort should go into the process of preparing and launching your book. It's an exciting time of celebration, and when you invite others to join you, it will not only be more satisfying, it will lead to book sales! Here's a list of some of the tasks involved in your launch. Feel free to modify this to suit your needs. You can download a printable copy here: http://nonfictionau-thorsassociation.com/book-downloads/.

PRE-LAUNCH TASKS

- Write sales copy for website
- Write sales copy for email
- Write sales copy for affiliates (if applicable)
- Write tweets and social media posts
- Set up shopping cart buttons with "thank you" text
- Set up discount codes (if applicable)
- Create a landing page on website
- Test landing page and purchase process, including product download link and email responders
- Write related blog posts to promote the book, which can include excerpts and related content
- Schedule blog posts to publish
- Schedule social media promotions
- Schedule email announcement(s) to mailing list
- Reach out to affiliates/JV partners

LAUNCH DAY TASKS

- Schedule the full day at your desk
- Double-check landing page and purchase process
- Announce to social media networks if not already scheduled
- Announce to online groups and forums
- Send a press release (if applicable)
- Send reminder emails to JV partners
- Report progress on social media networks throughout the day to build momentum
- Monitor email for questions/issues throughout the day

POST-LAUNCH DAY TASKS

- If campaign has a special offer or expiration date, send reminders via email

- Post expiration reminders to your social media networks

- Be responsive to your audience—respond to emails quickly

- Make a list of what worked and what didn't work so you can make adjustments for next time

Ask Your Contacts for Support

When planning your book launch, it's important to involve your contacts—friends, family, peers, and associates—and have them help you. I've met countless authors over the years who mention the many great contacts they have, but when the rubber hits the road and it's time for book promotion, often times those contacts are forgotten or ignored.

The thing about your contacts is that you can't expect them to know how to promote your book for you. If you want their help, you need to ask them to take action, and provide some direction for them to follow. It doesn't have to be invasive or painful in any way. In fact, many will be eager to help—but they can't do that until you let them know what you need.

Here are some ways your contacts can participate in book promotion:

- Send an announcement to their networks (be sure to send them short, medium, and long versions of sales copy so they can easily copy and paste)

- Recommend you as a speaker at their trade association or company

- Announce your book via social media (send a document with pre-written tweets and messages)

- Send a recommendation to specific individuals (this is different than sending an announcement to the masses—ask your contacts if they know anyone who would benefit from your book and invite them to forward along some details)

- Review your book on Amazon

- Review your book on a blog/website/radio show/publication

- Write about your book in a blog post

- List your book for sale on a website

- Purchase your books to give away to clients or employees

- Recommend your book to an organization that could benefit from purchasing copies

- Introduce you to a key contact or media source

This is just a partial list to get you started. Realize that different contacts can offer different benefits. I recommend making a spreadsheet that lists all of your key contacts and how each may be able to help you. Have this ready before your book launch campaign so that you know exactly who you will contact and how you will ask them to assist. Remember, if you wait for them to help, they may not know what to do or may forget to take action. Simply ask for what you need.

Amazon Bestseller Campaigns

You've probably heard about the Amazon Bestseller campaigns by now. This involves a process of collecting bonus items from alliance partners and having them help you announce and promote your book launch on the same day, with the goal of having your book reach #1 in a sub-category on Amazon.

The fact is that it's not hard to hit the top ten in a sub-category like this: *Nonfiction > Advice & How-to > Health, Mind & Body > Self-Help > **Happiness*** It also doesn't require that many book sales to reach the top of a sub-category. I know authors who've reached the top with as few as 20 books sold.

I don't like these campaigns for several reasons. First of all, the results are temporary. Sure you'll see a surge in sales on launch day, but that effort rarely leads to long-term results. Once the campaign is over, your book will fall back down the list and it will be as if the campaign never happened. These campaigns have also diluted the term "best seller." It used to be that authors could only claim bestselling status if their books hit a traditional list, such as *The New York Times* or *The Wall Street Journal*. Now nearly everyone with a book on Amazon can make this claim, and I find that rather disappointing.

I'd rather see authors focus on the marathon of marketing their books. After the frenzy dies down, you're still left to keep the promotion wheels turning. If you put your focus on a long-term strategy, the rewards will be much greater over time. One of my books, *From Entrepreneur to Infopreneur*, stayed in the top ten marketing books for small business for over two years. That was not the result of a manufactured campaign; it was due to an ongoing strategy to keep the book selling. I'd rather see you incorporate the strategies in this book to reach bigger and better goals.

Promote with Incentives

I mentioned in an earlier chapter that I am an advocate of giving incentives for book buyers. It's similar to a retailer offering a buy-one-get-one-free offer. In this case, your bonus item could be a companion workbook, templates or worksheets, or items that you collect from peers.

Instead of following the Amazon Bestseller Campaign route and giving bonuses away for a day or two, why not give them away for a month—or a year or more? It provides value for your readers, which can build loyalty, and it shouldn't cost you anything if your bonus items are delivered via electronic download. I used this strategy when I launched my last book, *Own Your Niche*. The bonus items were so well-received that I decided to leave the offer up indefinitely.

One of the smartest launch campaigns I've seen was when Colette Baron-Reid's book *The Map* was released. In lieu of incentives, buyers could enter to win dozens of prizes offered by the author's partners (fellow authors at Hay House publishing). There was an elaborate website set up where you could click on each contributor's link, which would add you to their mailing list and enter you to win a prize. Prizes ranged from tickets to a cruise to consulting sessions with the promotion partners.

I liked that this campaign was out of the box, and that it benefited all who participated. Baron-Reid's promotion partners benefited from lots of exposure and also grew their mailing lists. Participants had a chance to win prizes. This felt less contrived that one of the standard Amazon Bestseller campaigns, and the promotion also ran for several weeks, not just one day.

The point is to get creative with your launch strategy and make it a win-win for you and your readers.

Plan Your Launch Party

Planning a party to celebrate the release of your book, especially if it's your first book, can be a lot of fun. Writing a book is a big accomplishment and you deserve to celebrate that. There are many ways to approach a party. I've known authors who've hosted parties at their homes, in bars and restaurants, and in unexpected venues like a home improvement store.

If you want your launch party to generate sales and build some buzz, then your best bet is to hold it at a local bookstore. Most bookstores will gladly let you host your party there, even if you've self-published. They know that a launch party means that you will bring people into the store. As an added benefit, you can attract new buyers from those shopping in the store at the time.

If you're a new or self-published author, most stores will likely offer to sell your books for you on consignment (you won't handle your own sales in a retail establishment—they will want a piece of the action). The typical bookstore discount is 40%, which means the store takes 40% off of your retail price and pays you the other 60%. For large chain stores, your check will be issued 30 to 60 days later, and they might ask to keep a few copies on display after the party ends.

If you're going to host a public launch party, pay attention to the details. Bring in items to decorate a display table (the store will likely set up a bare table for you). Bring along your marketing collateral—bookmarks, postcards, etc. Also, make sure you have a way to get people to sign up for your mailing list. A simple basket or bowl for collecting business cards will do. You might serve cake, cupcakes, appetizers, or a simple bowl of candy. Balloons and signage can help draw attention, too.

Ask the store to help you promote the release in advance. One way you can make it easy for them is to offer to print up bag stuffers, which would involve a simple flyer announcing the book launch party. You can have four of them cut out of each 8.5x11 sheet of paper, and provide them to the store a couple of weeks in advance. The store will want them to look very professional, so be sure to include the store logo and get their approval before you invest in printing. You can also provide small posters for the store to display in advance if they are willing to do so.

At the launch party, plan something that will engage the crowd. You could give a reading from your book or a brief presentation. Better yet, give a brief talk at the top of each hour. Your party should last three or four hours so you can repeat your efforts. To add to the fun and encourage mailing list signups, you might hold drawings throughout the event where you give away prizes.

One of my clients, Bob Quinlan, author of *Earn It: Empower Yourself for Love*, went all out for his launch party. He held the event at a local chain bookstore and hired a band to play outside in the front of the store on a beautiful summer afternoon. The store was located in a busy strip mall, so the band drew a crowd all by itself. Next to the band was a table hosted by Bob's friends, where visitors could sign up for the mailing list and enter to win raffle prizes. He collected prizes from nearby businesses prior to the event.

Inside, in the middle of the store, Bob had a projector and screen, several dozen chairs set up for an audience, and a display table where he signed books. He gave several brief talks covering tips from his book throughout the afternoon. In the end, he sold over 100 books and the store manager was so impressed that he kept Bob's books on display in some prime store real estate for several months after the event was over.

Most important to a successful launch party is that you start by inviting your friends and family. When you build your crowd, others will follow. They will want to know what all the fuss is about. So invite them to join you and don't forget to take lots of pictures of you in action, signing your books, and enjoying the crowd. Those will make great shots to share on your website and social media.

How to Autograph Books

Awhile back a new author asked me how she should handle autographing her books. It took me back to when I had published my first book, remembering how awkward it felt to sign copies. I also thought about my first business—a bookstore—where we flipped through used books in search of autographs (the equivalent of hitting a literary jackpot!). Some were short and sweet with just a name, while others had more personal inscriptions. I wrote the following as a blog post on AuthorityPublishing.com, and to date it is the single most visited page on the site! Who knew?

Here are some simple tips to help you prepare to autograph your books:

1. **Decide where to sign.** I like to sign my books on the title page, which is where most books are autographed, though you can also

sign the inside cover. In some cases, you may want to sign the front cover, though this is rare and would probably only be appropriate for a coffee table book or something that will be on display.

2. **Personalize your message.** In most cases people want the book inscribed to them personally, though sometimes it's intended as a gift so be sure to ask, "Should I sign this to you?" Use their first name and <u>always ask for the spelling</u> since even common names can have unusual spellings.

 If you have time, try to personalize your message in some way: "It was great meeting you at the XYZ conference" or "I enjoyed learning about your business…"

3. **Choose your signature phrase.** Ideally you should have one to three phrases that you write each time you sign a book so you don't have to think too hard! Your message can also be memorable and should fit within the space allotted.

 When I'm not pressed for time, I sign my books: "Wishing you abundant joy and success." If a line of people are waiting I simply write "Best wishes." Here are some others:

- All my best
- Thanks
- In gratitude
- To your health
- To your success
- Much appreciation
- Warm wishes
- Best regards
- Onward
- Your friend
- Love
- Cheers to you

- Be happy
- Stay brilliant

4. **Make sure your name is legible.** Consider the fact that someday your book could be a collector's item! Even if it isn't, do you want to leave any doubt that you're the one who signed it? If needed, practice writing your name so that it is at least partially legible. You should also sign first and last name unless your name is Madonna or Cher.

5. **Add a date (optional).** Admittedly, I usually omit the date—mostly because I can never remember what day it is! But recipients do appreciate it when you date your inscription.

6. **Use a good pen.** I'll never forget the day I was signing books and the only pen I had with me was one of those cheap stick pens I picked up from a hotel room. Though it got the job done, it certainly didn't demonstrate how serious I am about my work.

For those of you who autograph the cover or inside cover, a good Sharpie will probably be your best choice. For everyone else, do yourself a favor and invest in a nice pen. It doesn't matter if the ink is blue or black, if the barrel is thick or thin, just choose something that you love and that makes you feel like an author! (Oh, and make sure the ink dries quickly!)

Author Interview

Name: Michelle Dunn

Websites: www.Credit-and-Collections.com (blog) http://michelledunn. com/mmblog/ (marketing blog) www.MichelleDunn.com (website)

Books:

- *Starting a Collection Agency*
- *Become the Squeaky Wheel*
- *The Ultimate Credit and Collections Handbook*
- *The Guide to Getting Paid*

- *Credit and Collections: A Business Perspective*
- *Mosquito Marketing for Authors*
- *Marketing Plan for a Medical Collection Agency*

I am also in the process of writing "Marketing for Collection Agencies" which will be released this year.

Are you traditionally published or self-published, and why did you make that choice?

I am traditionally published and self-published. I started out self-publishing because when I wrote my first book I was also running my business and felt I did not have time to write and send out proposals to publishers and felt an urgency to get my book published and out to my pre-order list. Once I became a successful self-published author, I had publishers sending me contracts, which prompted me to get an agent to help me deal with them and choose the best one.

Most recently, my second hardcover book was published by Cambridge Scholars Publishing: *Credit and Collections, A Business Perspective,* and I released a self-published Kindle book called *Telephone Collection Call Scripts & How to Respond to Excuses.*

Who is your target audience of readers?

My target audience is business owners and entrepreneurs. Anyone who extends credit to customers, anyone who has past due customers and anyone who wants a better customer base and wants to limit their credit risk and make more money.

What has been the single most effective marketing strategy you have used for promoting your book?

My most effective marketing strategy has been to only market to my target audience and relevant publications, magazines or newspapers. Really focusing on my niche has helped me sell more books, by networking with them, answering their questions on my discussion groups online, and by writing my columns. Another effective marketing strategy for me has been using Amazon's KDP program and being able to offer some of my titles free to my readers, this resulting in more sales of my books that were not free and new customers as well as some random reviews for my books.

What are some other marketing tactics that have or haven't worked for you?

Things that have not worked for me are sending out press releases blindly to any publication, or marketing to an audience that doesn't extend credit or have customers that owe them money. Paying for an ad in the newspaper or a magazine turned out to be a big waste of money. Submitting articles or being interviewed for a story was much more effective.

How has social media impacted your success? Which social media networks do you feel generate the best results for you?

Social media has impacted my success; it has helped me reach an audience I may not have reached otherwise. It has allowed me to network with others in my industry and customers, especially at a time when my finances were tight and I could not attend as many industry events or shows. Being active on social media has helped me sell more books, increase my mailing list and customer base, and has gotten me speaking gigs, radio and print interviews and new joint ventures. I use LinkedIn and also have two groups there, Starting a Collection Agency and The Guide to Getting Paid. I also use Twitter and have a Facebook page for my books. I feel that LinkedIn works best for me and my books since it is a more business-oriented social network and my books are business books and my target audience is businesses.

What have been some of the biggest benefits of publishing a book?

The biggest benefit for me from publishing my books is being able to share what I know about what I do and my experiences and making money from it. I sold my business to write full time, so I spend much of my time writing new books and promoting existing books. I am trying to create passive income so I can do other things and not "work" so much in credit and collections. Publishing a book also pushed me up into "expert" status according to the media, which is great for my book sales as well.

What advice would you offer to new authors who are getting ready to promote their books?

My advice for a new author getting ready to promote their book is to write a marketing plan! I write a marketing plan for every single book I put out - even if it is a short Kindle book. Even if you just have one page, having a plan can help you tremendously. Also, focus on where your target audience is and put yourself in front of them, the groups they are members of, online and offline, the newspapers or magazines they read; you want to give them information they can use, not preach about how great your book is. If you can share helpful information that hooks your reader they will want to know more, and therefore need to buy your book. Once your book is published, ask for reviews. Most folks say yes. Use those reviews to promote your book and ask that person for referrals. You have to let people know about your book and what it can do for them; focus on the benefits your book will bring your audience.

If you were starting over today, is there anything you would do differently?

I don't think I would do anything differently; I have been self-published and traditionally published and have to say I like being self-published more, though I do like the credibility being traditionally published brings you as an author. I have enjoyed my publishing journey and am looking forward to publishing more myself, though last year I was approached by a publisher and that could happen again this year! I won't turn down a paying book offer!

Is there anything else you would like to add?

I would like to add that it is discouraging being an author marketing your books. Most authors know how to write, not how to market, so educate yourself. Read all you can on book marketing and talk to others who have done it or are doing it now. Every single day do at least one thing to market your book so you don't get overwhelmed, and have a marketing plan, no matter how short it is, it will help keep you on track.

Chapter 5:
Publicity and the Media

*"I've learned that people will forget what you said, people
will forget what you did, but people will never forget
how you made them feel."*
– Maya Angelou

OPEN ANY NEWSPAPER OR MAGAZINE and notice how each article includes quotes and advice from experts. Most often, these quotes come from authors. Tune in to any talk radio show, *The Today Show*, or even your local news programs. Authors are constantly in the spotlight. In fact, media professionals from print, radio and television frequently search Amazon.com for authors of books related to their needed subject matter.

There is a reason the word "authority" begins with "author." Having a book published makes you an instant authority on your subject matter, and a logical source for media interviews. Gaining media coverage should be a top priority for every author because when your book is mentioned in a major media outlet, it will inevitably attract readers.

What You Need to Know Before You Pitch the Media

You should know that reporters, editors, and producers NEED story ideas. In other words, *they need you as much as you need them*. Yes, it's perfectly okay to reach out to media pros, and in fact they want compelling story ideas. Though before you do, make sure you have a news-worthy pitch. A new book release doesn't usually qualify as news-worthy, especially considering there are hundreds of thousands of new book titles released each year, unless your book is relevant to something currently happening in the news. Instead, tie your pitch into a topic that is *timely*. When you can tie your story idea into something relevant that's happening in the news such as a holiday (Valentine's Day), event (like the Olympics), or other current trend (Pinterest, anyone?), that can grab attention.

For example, if your book is about creating a happy marriage, you could send a pitch two to three weeks before Valentine's Day with a list of Ten Ways to Keep Romance Alive. This is the kind of pitch that will get scooped up by local newspapers and morning news shows. At tax time, accountants and bookkeepers get interviewed. When school ends for summer break, all kinds of experts provide tips for pool safety, things to do with kids, summer vacation ideas, and strategies to keep your kids reading while on break.

You can also get coverage by tying your expertise into a current event. For example, after Lance Armstrong confessed to doping during his career, body language experts were featured on many news outlets discussing whether he seemed honest and sincere. Whenever a major celebrity gets in trouble, addiction experts, psychologists and psychiatrists are interviewed. When there is a major company scandal, such as what happened with Enron several years ago, financial advisors and stock market professionals are interviewed.

The reality is that you are an authority in your subject matter and you can find ways to be relevant to media outlets. To get the best results, figure out how to be newsworthy. All the media outlets want to deliver timely, relevant information to their audiences. Your job is to make that easy for them by stepping up to answer questions that are in the minds of their audience.

Press Releases

The old standard for public relations (PR) is to send a press release. These days many authors use services such as PRWeb.com, a paid distribution service. However, the results you'll see from online press release distribution are most often disappointing. Media professionals rarely pay attention to these releases. The biggest benefit you'll enjoy from an online service is that it will likely draw traffic to your website, which is not a bad thing.

For better results with press releases, you should send yours directly to reporters, editors, and producers. Most media outlets accept releases via email these days and list a general email address on their website. But you can take that a step further and send your release directly to the reporter, editor or producer who you feel would be a good fit for your pitch.

If you're going to send a press release, make sure it looks as professional as possible. It should have a compelling headline, contact information, and the first paragraph should cover the five W's: who, what, when, where, and why. Keep it brief and to the point. Search PRWeb.com for some strong examples to emulate.

How to Build a List of Media Contacts

I can assure you that you will have far more success reaching out to media contacts directly. Here's how to find them.

Media Websites

Nearly all of the major media outlets have websites with easy access to contact information for reporters, editors, and producers. In fact, they make it almost ridiculously easy to find email information because they need story ideas! While this information is easy to locate, the research can take time. You should always start with local media, since being a local resident will help you get coverage. Look for contacts at newspapers, magazines, morning news shows, and talk radio. Also, look for national reporters whose work you are familiar with and who you think would be likely to write the story you want to pitch.

Media Lists

You can skip all the time-consuming research and buy a media list. Two reputable sources: Cision's media database, formerly Bacon's (http://us.cision.com/index.asp) and Gebbie Press (http://gebbiepress.com).

LinkedIn

Just about anyone who is anyone is on LinkedIn now. You can use the Advanced Search feature to locate users by keywords, company name, publication name, or job title. If you're not yet connected, you'll need to either request an introduction from a mutual friend or pay to upgrade your LinkedIn account so that you can email contacts outside of your network. You can also track down a contact name, return to Google, and search for an email address.

Google

Use the search engine to search for media sources. For example, if you want to reach media in your old hometown, you can search Google for "newspaper

Indianapolis," "news Indianapolis," "radio Indianapolis," etc. You can also search for terms like "list of weekly newspapers." Smaller publications like hometown magazines and newspapers are great sources for getting coverage.

Be on the Lookout

Whether you're surfing social media or reading a magazine in your doctor's office lobby, keep an eye out for reporters who write about topics related to what you do. Most reporters have a specialty area of focus. If a reporter writes about the stock market, he probably won't be writing about the latest in cake decorating, so find the reporters who can connect with your message and reach out. Even if you're simply offering a compliment on a great story with a quick note that says you're available as a source if the reporter writes a follow-up article, you have opened up a line of communication. It might sound crazy, but reporters have databases of contacts and you never know when you might rise from the archives.

Build Rapport

Reporters are like any other business contact. You can build and maintain a relationship with them over time. If you prove to be a good source for interviews, there is a very good chance the reporter will reach out to you again in the future. And you can also contact the reporter again several months later. Remind him that you contributed to a previous article and send another pitch. I maintain relationships with several reporters both locally and nationally. It's a mutually beneficial relationship since they know they can rely on me to respond quickly and deliver useful answers, and in turn I get repeat coverage in various publications. You can even become a regular guest on your local morning news program by serving as the local health expert or clutter clearing resource. If you do your job well and get to know the producers and reporters, you can get invited back several times each year.

Pitch the Media Directly

While press releases are the old PR standard, one very effective way to get media coverage is to reach out to media pros directly via email. Once again, these folks need story ideas. When you send a brief, relevant, professional pitch via email, you are quite likely to get a call back.

When sending a pitch via email, keep it brief. Reporters, editors, and producers are busy people who receive a lot of emails. They scan emails quickly and are used to hitting the delete key, so get to your point right away. It doesn't hurt to mention familiarity with their work, too. A simple paragraph or two with a compelling pitch works best. Here's an example:

> Dear Joe,
>
> I recently came across your article about how retailers are using Facebook to get more customers and I thought it was really well done. With National Small Business Week approaching (May 21-25), I wanted to propose an article on new ways that small businesses are benefiting from Pinterest. As you may have heard, Pinterest is now the third largest social media network based on the number of visitors. I am the author of *XYZ Social Media Guide* and I'd love to share with you some concrete examples and strategies that your readers can use to promote their businesses on Pinterest during Small Business Week.
>
> Thank you very much for your consideration.
>
> Best wishes,
>
> Susie
> <contact information, including phone number and email address>

Here are some considerations to keep in mind:

Newspapers – Depending on when they are published, newspaper reporters need content daily or weekly, which means they are always on the hunt for compelling stories. Make sure you contact the right reporter for your topic. If your pitch is about Small Business Week, don't waste the Lifestyle reporter's time.

Magazines – Depending on the circulation size, magazines have a much longer lead time before going to press. That means that they usually run three to six months ahead of schedule. If you want to pitch your book as an ideal holiday gift, you should start in July.

Local Newspapers and Magazines – Always start by building your media portfolio locally. It's far easier to get local coverage than national coverage, and often times the larger publications pay attention to stories from smaller publications, so you never know what opportunities can arise later. Also, your hometown newspaper may syndicate some of its content nationally.

Local TV News – Provided you can craft your pitch to fit in with the tone of your local programming, this can be a great way to build local exposure.

National TV News – It's often easier to go national after you've landed some local coverage. The bigger shows like *Good Morning America* and *The Today Show* want to see clips and know that you are a good bet to have on air.

Radio – Most authors should focus on the news talk radio programs, such as NPR. Most radio interviews are brief (5 to 10 minutes), unless you're invited into the studio to chat with a host for a longer period. The great thing about radio is you don't have to be local—you can call in to stations across the country. Make sure you have access to a good land line.

50 Reasons to Contact the Media

1. Comment on industry trend
2. Holiday tie-in
3. Piggyback on breaking news
4. Industry statistics
5. Contest launch
6. Contest results
7. A contest you've won
8. Announce a new book, product or service
9. Innovative use for your product or service
10. Off-the-wall promotion
11. Special event
12. Comment on news story
13. Charitable contribution
14. Fundraiser you're hosting
15. Fundraiser you're sponsoring

16. Demonstration with broad appeal (i.e. cooking, organizing)

17. Award received

18. Free samples/giveaways

19. Free demonstrations

20. Free classes/events

21. Company anniversary

22. Industry predictions

23. Survey/research launch

24. Survey/research results

25. Alliance/joint venture with another company

26. Tips round-up

27. Release a new whitepaper or special report

28. Announce new patents

29. Community involvement

30. Partnership with celebrity

31. Open house

32. Company executive to appear at event

33. Incorporation change or IPO

34. New employees or officers

35. Change or launch of board of directors

36. Financial reports

37. Grants you're giving or receiving

38. Scholarships you're giving

39. Sponsorships (i.e. local sports team or Super Bowl)

40. Media coverage received

41. Participation in local events

42. Business expansion

43. Classes or workshops

44. Mergers and acquisitions

45. Take a position on a political issue

46. New location/facilities

47. Authored a book

48. Mentioned in a book

49. Appointment to a board or committee

50. Changes to policies/procedures

Media Training for Authors

I will never forget what happened after sending out my first press release after opening my first business, a bookstore in Sacramento, California. I didn't know much about what I was doing at the time, so I wrote the release and sent it off to several media outlets. Then I went to the mall.

My phone rang while I was in the dressing room at Macy's. It was a reporter who was prepared to interview me on the spot. I sat down and as we chatted, I realized that I was completely unprepared. I hadn't anticipated her questions and therefore, my answers rambled.

I learned some lessons the hard way, and since then I've been through actual media training (a worthwhile investment if you can afford it), where I practiced interviews on camera and learned how to give compelling answers. Here are some tips so you can be prepared when the media calls:

1. **Anticipate questions.** Develop a list of potential questions you think a reporter would ask you and then write down your responses, ideally in simple bullet points so that your answers are concise. Reporters want quick, thoughtful answers.

2. **Know what messages you want to convey.** Though you might end up answering questions for 15 minutes, it's likely that only a few of your quotes will end up in the story. Every comment counts so make sure each answer has impact. Also, have a goal in mind for the interview. Do you want to promote your latest book, mention an upcoming event, or draw attention to a promotion you are running? You will need to find an eloquent way to mention anything promotional since media pros aren't there to help you promote your business. They want concrete information. Any mention of your book or business will almost be an afterthought so tread carefully.

3. **Be prepared. For radio and TV, there's little or no editing.** Everything you say is recorded for all eternity. All the more reason to know your key messages, practice them, say them out loud in the car, have your kids interview you at the dinner table—whatever it takes to always be ready.

4. **Talk in sound bites.** The media likes short answers that are to the point, especially on radio and TV. Questions come in rapid-fire fashion and your answers should keep up with the pace. Your answers may end up becoming part of a promotional clip so responses should be confident and clear. Pay attention to how professionals handle interviews on the big morning shows and learn by their examples.

5. **Be available for at least a week after sending out a press release.** Don't go on vacation or disappear for several days. If a reporter calls and leaves a message, call back as soon as humanly possible. There are always deadlines involved. I learned this one the hard way when my son was home sick and I failed to check my voicemail until the next day. I missed a great opportunity; the reporter had already moved on and found another source.

6. **Have fun with interviews.** You want to be prepared without sounding like a robot. Let your personality shine through and make the reporter's job easy. When you're a good interview subject, it is quite likely you will be contacted by that reporter again in the future.

7. **Thank the reporter after the interview.** Reporters, editors and producers do not get enough appreciation for what they do and when you take time to send a quick note, it will be noticed and remembered. Reporters need a lot of sources and they are people, too. Show

that you are a great source and you can build a relationship that endures.

Get Found By Media Pros

More than half of the media interviews I've given over the years came to me without any effort on my part. Why? Because I have positioned myself as an authority.

Many interviews have come from reporters who found my blog. When the recession was just starting, I wrote several blog posts about how I was going to do business in the recession (a timely topic that every news outlet was frantically covering). That's when I learned that reporters, editors, and producers use Google to find sources. They would locate my blog, discover that I was also an author, and that led to numerous interviews with print, radio and television. I even ended up giving a live interview to *Sunrise 7*, Australia's version of *The Today Show*. They featured me as the U.S. representative for what was happening in the small business economy!

Just last week I gave an interview to a reporter who found my books on Amazon. My books have attracted many interviews like this one. Reporters absolutely search Amazon to find sources to interview.

I've also been interviewed by reporters who found me on Twitter. One way to boost your chances of getting found by reporters is to follow them on Twitter first! You can search Google and Twitter to find many media professionals. Another great place to locate media pros on Twitter is via http://muckrack.com. By following them, the hope is that they will follow you back and pay attention to your activity. You can also tweet them directly to compliment a story or offer additional thoughts on a story.

To position yourself as an authority who gets found for media interviews, begin building your media portfolio. Remember to update the Media page on your website. Demonstrate that you are an experienced and reliable source. If you are consistently promoting your work online, you will begin to attract these types of opportunities.

Help a Reporter Out

Help a Reporter (http://helpareporter.com) is a public relations service that connects media professionals with sources. Three times per day, emails are sent out to subscribers featuring queries (interview requests) from reporters, producers, and bloggers like me.

Recently I sent out a request for interviews with entrepreneurs and business book authors for my blog and received over 200 responses. Fabulous! What wasn't so fabulous was how many responses I had to delete.

In my query, I specifically asked respondents to send one paragraph describing their business or book. Instead, I received an influx of essays and canned company descriptions copied and pasted by PR firms. I waded through 200 messages, growing more annoyed with the laziness of the responses and the inability to follow a simple direction.

One surprising revelation was that some people feel that it is no longer important in society to write in full sentences. Apparently we can simply ignore capitalization, punctuation and complete words and instead submit a media response as if answering a text message!

Hello! LOL OMG WTH?

Oh, and my favorites were the ones who sent a link to "learn more about me here." No supporting text, no single paragraph as requested, just a link.

I also received responses from:

- People who formerly owned a business
- People who claimed to own multiple businesses but failed to mention what any of them were
- Aspiring authors who hadn't yet published
- One schmuck who repeatedly asked me to review his product
- PR firms that provided an extensive list of clients they deemed appropriate
- A surprising number of PR firms who pitched themselves as sources! (Can't say I blame them, though.)

If you want to get interviews from HARO requests, follow the directions of the media pro. If asked to send a single paragraph, do that. Make it interesting and get to the point. I'll also add that those who made a point of connecting with me, mentioning my books or articles, or reaching out via Twitter also caught my attention. Reporters get inundated with HARO responses and it's actually pretty easy to stand out if you respond as requested.

AUTHOR TIP: Another resource for attracting media interviews is http://profnet.com, a professional network where subscribers can feature a profile that covers their credentials and receive inquiries from reporters. This service comes with a price tag, but most authors I know who have participated have reported good results.

Contact Internet Media Sources

While authors should certainly work to get traditional media coverage, there are just as many opportunities to get publicity through Internet media sources.

Bloggers

Bloggers have more influence than ever before. Consumers love recommendations, especially on what books to read, so reaching out to bloggers can lead to some tremendous exposure. Some things to keep in mind when contacting bloggers:

- The top bloggers receive a lot of pitches. You might get better results by pitching to mid-level bloggers who still have loyal readers but aren't quite as inundated with requests.

- Make sure your pitch fits the tone of the blog. If you're asking for a book review, search the blog to see if other book reviews have been featured there. If not, find another angle. Perhaps you could offer up copies of your book as a giveaway promotion or contribute a guest article.

- Get creative and try to create a win-win situation. For example, you could offer to feature the blogger on your site in exchange for a mention on her site. Or you could offer to promote the blogger to your social media following.

- Flattery will get you everywhere. Make sure you let the blogger know that you enjoy their work and that you're familiar with their content.

To locate bloggers, search for keywords related to the topic of your book via http://technorati.com, http://networkedblogs.com, http://blogarama.com, or http://bloghub.com.

Social Media Influencers

Much like bloggers, social media influencers are people with large social media followings. You can find them by searching social media sites directly including Facebook, Twitter, Google+, LinkedIn and Pinterest. You will need to be creative with pitches to these folks. Most will also have active blogs so research them a bit to figure out the best approach. Consider offering up a contest suggestion or book giveaway.

Internet Radio Shows

Radio interviews are one of my favorite promotion strategies for authors. Aside from the fact that you can almost always conduct them from home, you can also reach a broad audience with your message.

Internet radio shows, such as those found at BlogTalkRadio.com, provide wonderful opportunities for authors to reach a niche audience. Here you can find shows covering everything from business blogging to parenting. Shows typically feature guests for 15 minutes up to a full hour. Guests are typically promoted online before and after the show, and the recording of your appearance will often be loaded to iTunes and can remain online for years.

Sending a simple email can be quite effective for booking these interviews. Here's a sample I put together to show you how to craft yours.

Greetings <first name>,

My name is Stephanie Chandler and I am the author of *Booked Up! How to Write, Publish, and Promote a Book to Grow Your Business*. I have reviewed your show archives and I believe that I would be a great guest for your audience.

Proposed Topic: Marketing your business by writing and publishing books and ebooks.

Did you know that a recent survey showed that more than 80% of Americans would like to write a book? At the same time, businesses are looking for new marketing strategies and ways to stay competitive in a challenging economy. Promoting a business with a book can be a powerful way to gain a competitive advantage, and it's easier to accomplish than you might think.

As a guest on your show, I can discuss the following key points:

- How businesses can use books for marketing purposes.
- Simple strategies for writing a book quickly.
- Publishing options including traditional and self-publishing.
- Ways to produce ebooks for the Kindle, iPhone, iPad, Nook and more.
- Methods for building buzz online.

I have years of experience as a radio show guest and I can assure you that our time together will be well-spent and focused on delivering value to your audience. I would also be happy to provide you with sample interview questions and a complimentary copy of my book at your request.

Thank you very much for your consideration. I look forward to hearing back from you.

Warm regards,

Stephanie Chandler

<insert contact information: email, phone, website URL>

Some additional considerations:

- Always address the host or producer by name when sending your pitch.
- Write a compelling introduction that captures interest.
- Provide a simple list of three to five key discussion points.
- Mention previous interview experience since it increases confidence of the host or producer and lets them know you'll be a good guest. If you don't have previous experience, assure the host that your goal

is to provide an informative interview for his/her audience.

- Offer to provide sample interview questions. Radio hosts may or may not use them, but it demonstrates professionalism to provide them. Make a list of eight to fifteen questions that you think the audience might like to know. Put these in a nicely formatted document and include a brief bio (that will likely be read on-air) and your contact information. You can download a sample media sheet here: http://nonfictionauthorsassociation.com/book-downloads/.

- Offer a complimentary copy of your book for review. This can help hook the producer or host and give them more reasons to talk about your book on air.

To locate shows, spend some time on Google and search directories such as http://blogtalkradio.com, http://alltalkradio.net, http://wsradio.com, and http://womensradio.com. Also, search through podcasts on iTunes to find podcast programs that reach your target audience.

To save you time, we also sell lists of Internet radio shows here: http://authoritypublishing.com/store/internet-radio-shows-and-podcasts-lists/.

Virtual Book Tours

A virtual book tour is a promotion where you set a specified time, usually two to four weeks, and you put yourself on "tour." The idea is to get other blogs to feature you each day during your tour stops. Blog hosts might feature a guest blog post by you, a review of your book, or a written interview. In exchange, you should share a link back to the host blog on your own site and across your social media networks.

To create a virtual book tour, start by finding appropriate blog sites and then reach out and ask if they would be interested in featuring you during your tour. Most bloggers are familiar with this concept and many will oblige because the benefits are mutual. It's also a good idea to offer the blog host a complimentary copy of your book. This shows goodwill, plus it may hook the blogger and inspire them to write more about your book at a later date.

You can also spend some time with Google searches to locate blogs that have featured virtual book tour stops. It will take some work to compile a list of contacts and reach out to them. This is a great task to assign to a virtual assistant.

As a side note, virtual book tours are another area where I personally don't follow the rules. Rather than putting myself on tour for a few weeks, I believe that I am always on tour. I don't set a specific time frame for these events, and instead focus on finding opportunities year-round. Do what feels right for you!

Author Interview

Name: Hal Elrod

Website: www.MiracleMorning.com

Books:

- *Taking Life Head On: How To Love the Life You Have While You Create the Life of Your Dreams*
- *The Miracle Morning: The Not-So-Obvious Secret Guaranteed To Transform Your Life… (Before 8AM)*

Are you traditionally published or self-published, and why did you make that choice?

Despite entertaining offers from traditional publishers, I opted to self-publish both of my books. While there are many reasons, the ones that most influenced my decision were maintaining the rights to my intellectual property (since I've got spin-off products and programs related to the title and subject matter of my book), being able to purchase bulk quantities of my books at a much lower price (since I sell them in the back of the room after my speeches), as well as keeping a higher percentage of my royalties.

Tell us a bit about your most recent book:

The Miracle Morning: The Not-So-Obvious Secret Guaranteed To Transform Your Life… (Before 8AM) is a #1 bestseller and has already sold over 9,000 copies (in the first two months) as well as garnered 77 Amazon Reviews (average of 4.9 stars).

The essence of the book is teaching people how to finally *wake up* to their full potential, by giving them a specialized morning routine to start their day off with, which increases motivation, clarity, as well as emotional and physical well-being.

Before it was a book, *The Miracle Morning*™ is something I shared with my coaching clients, as well as over 10,000 people through various online formats. Having received hundreds of emails from individuals stating that *The Miracle Morning*™ had positively impacted or transformed their life more than anything they had ever attempted before, I was compelled to share it in the form of a book. I'm beyond grateful to see the impact continue to grow as I read the ongoing reviews on Amazon, continue to receive success stories from people via email social media.

Who is your target audience of readers?

My target audience is really the self-help/personal development niche, as well as sales and business. Although, *The Miracle Morning*™ is in the process of becoming a book series (much like *Chicken Soup for the Soul©*) and with *The Miracle Morning*™ *For Christians* and *The Miracle Morning*™ *For Realtors* currently being written (with dozens of other titles being planned), my audience will continue to broaden.

What has been the single most effective marketing strategy you have used for promoting your book?

Creating an opt-in webpage where people can go to get free value (two chapters of the book, as well as a video training, and an audio training) at MiracleMorning.com. This exposed thousands of people to *The Miracle Morning*™ before the book was even written, as well as collected their email addresses so that I could continue to build a relationship with them and give them updates on the book, ultimately leading up to thousands of book buyers anxiously awaiting its release.

What are some other marketing tactics that have or haven't worked for you?

I wrote an article in Jeffrey Gitomer's "Sales Caffeine" ezine, which drove 4,500 people to my blog at www.MiracleMorningBlog.com. However, looking back I should have sent them to my opt-in page at MiracleMorning.com, because of those 4,500 new visitors, I only captured about 10% of their names and emails, as my blog isn't focused on that task. As a result, over 4,000 of those 4,500 visitors may or may not ever find me again.

I also followed the steps in Michael Hyatt's blog, particularly his instructions for creating my Launch Team, which can be found at http://michaelhyatt.com/bestseller-launch-formula.html.

How has social media impacted your success? Which social media networks do you feel generate the best results for you?

Social media has been a key component is spreading the word (and getting others to spread the word) about not only my book, but even more important has been driving traffic to my opt-in webpage, to build my list.

I personally prefer Facebook (although my Facebook posts automatically and simultaneously post to Twitter), and my strategy is to post "added value" communications, such as a motivational quote (almost always an original of mine) and then encourage people to click the "SHARE" button to pay it forward and add value to someone else's life. I often create a full-color JPEG image of the quote so it's more visually stimulating, which I have found to significantly increase the number of "shares" I get. You can see examples on my Facebook fan page at http://www.facebook.com/YoPalHal.

What have been some of the biggest benefits of publishing a book?

Personally, the greatest reward is receiving emails (or reading Amazon reviews) from people emphatically expressing appreciation for the impact that one of my books has made in their life.

Professionally, my books have led to highly paid speaking engagements ($3,500-$5,500), private coaching clients, opportunities such as TV interviews, and credibility that allows me to reach out and develop relationships with fellow authors and experts.

What advice would you offer to new authors who are getting ready to promote their books?

Two things I would recommend doing ASAP:

1. Create an opt-in webpage that gives away the first chapter or two of your book. I use Kajabi.com to create all of my opt-in pages (as well as membership sites where individuals pay an average of $97/month). This way, you can start building your opt-in email list and have other people share the link to your opt-in page via email and social media.

2. Create your Launch Team. Considering how lonely it can feel to be a solo author promoting your book, I can't tell you how valuable it was to have a group of people who believed in my message and were excited to share it with others! Again, I modeled the Launch Team strategy taught in Michael Hyatt's blog.

If you were starting over today, is there anything you would do differently?

I would have hired a coach to hold me accountable to finish *The Miracle Morning*™ book. I worked on it "alone" for over four years without even coming close to finishing it. When I finally hired a coach to help me gain clarity and hold me accountable, I finished it in four months. So, I was able to accomplish more in four months *with a coach* than I was in four years trying to do it on my own.

Is there anything else you would like to add?

Make sure you make your book available on Kindle the same day that it's available in print. I sell more of my books in Kindle format than any other.

Chapter 6:
Boost Sales on Amazon

"People who are crazy enough to think they can change the world, are the ones who do."
– Apple Inc.

THE REALITY THAT ALL authors must face is that the vast majority of book sales happen on Amazon.com. Unfortunately, this is putting our brick and mortar bookstores out of business, and also making them less relevant for generating book sales. If you're self-published, you may soon develop a love-hate relationship with Amazon. Some of their policies can be frustrating for publishers (like how they dictate pricing for ebooks). But since the majority of book sales happen on Amazon, it is important to learn how to make this mammoth retailer work in your favor.

It's equally important to know that just because your book is available on Amazon, doesn't mean readers will find it or make a decision to buy. There are a number of tactics you can use to help boost sales.

Create an Author Central Account

Amazon gives authors a fair amount of control and exposure by allowing you to create a free Author Central account: http://authorcentral.amazon.com/. As soon as your book is published and available on Amazon, you should create your account immediately.

Once you launch your account and claim your book(s), you can build out your author profile by including your photo, bio, a link to your blog feed (which will automatically display your recent blog posts), videos, event announcements, and Twitter feed. Your author profile link will be featured on your book's sales page, allowing visitors to learn more about you.

Another important benefit of the Author Central account is that you can also view your sales history. Amazon aggregates sales data from Book

Scan, and will show you the number of units sold each month, along with the geographic region where those sales occurred. Not all sales are reported here, for example sales in some brick and mortar stores will not appear here, but it will give you a good idea of your book's sales history on Amazon.

Boost Content on Your Book Page

Often times the description submitted with a book to Amazon gets squished up on the page and just doesn't look good. From your Author Central account, you can format the description and add additional detail. You can also share a note from the author, reviews, and other details. For my last book, I chose to publish the entire Table of Contents in the "From the Author" section, adding more keywords to my book page to improve search, and giving page visitors a clear view of the contents. Whatever you do here, take full advantage of the opportunity to expand the details on your book page to better capture the interest of potential readers.

Amazon Book Pricing and the Used Book Network

Amazon is known for its low prices and there is a good chance it will discount your book's retail price, especially if the book is selling well. The pricing Amazon chooses for your book can also change periodically. A $20 book might be listed for $18.59 one week and $16.50 another week. There is nothing you can do to affect this price and it doesn't change your compensation from Amazon—they still purchase your books at the wholesale price you or your publisher have set with them (usually 40% to 55% off of retail).

You may also notice that your book is listed for sale from third-party sellers in the New and Used categories. This can be alarming to new authors, especially when you haven't yet generated enough sales to have used copies in circulation. What happens most often here is that small independent booksellers have listed your book for sale. They have access to Ingram, which is the largest supplier of books to bookstores. If your book is available through Ingram (and it will be if you've published with a reputable publisher), then other booksellers can list your book in Amazon's marketplace and then drop-ship it from Ingram if and when it sells.

These third parties often try to compete with Amazon by pricing your book even lower than Amazon's list price. If your book sells through a third-party, you still earn revenue from the sale when it is reported back from

Ingram. And you may actually find that your book is listed in independent bookstore sites across the Internet because they are able to drop-ship from Ingram. Unfortunately, these booksellers don't have to buy your book before they list it and they are just pulling data from Ingram's catalog, but at least you are still compensated when a copy sells.

Understanding Sales Rank on Amazon

On every book page on Amazon is a sales rank number, and you'll likely become obsessed with yours. Nobody knows for sure how that ranking equates to exact book sales figures, but the lower the ranking, the better your book is selling.

Amazon updates the sales rank number each hour, so you might login at 8 a.m. and have a sales rank of 100,000, and then by noon it's changed to around 70,000. Unfortunately that doesn't mean your book has sold 30k copies, but it may have sold one or two. If your rank is 70,000, then there are 69,999 books selling better than yours. If your rank is 10, then there are just 9 books selling better than yours across the site.

Legend has it that Amazon resets this ranking every 60 to 90 days in order to keep books visible. So if your book didn't sell any copies for 90 days, the ranking would plummet to a number greater than 100k or even 1million. Because of this, it's important to maintain at least a small number of sales—at least 5 copies per week—to keep the ranking under 100k.

According to a report from rampant-books.com, here are what sales numbers *may* equate to (nobody knows for sure):

Amazon Sales Rank	Actual Books Sold Per Week
75-100	250-275/week
100-200	225-249/week
200-300	150-200/week
450-750	75-100/week
750-3,000	40-75/week
3,000-9,000	15-20/week
10,000+	1-5/week

Amazon also ranks books by sub-category, which indicates how popular a book is within its given category. For example, here's an actual ranking for a business book on Amazon:

Amazon Best Sellers Rank: #7,996 in Books

#21 in Books > Business & Investing > Industries & Professions > **E-commerce**

#80 in Books > Business & Investing > Small Business & Entrepreneurship > **Entrepreneurship**

Based on the chart above, this book is likely selling 15 to 20 copies per week, which is enough for it to rank as #21 in the E-commerce sub-category. This can be beneficial since browsers who are interested in this category and search for titles will stumble across this one when viewing the top 100 list for that category.

Here is an example from a book in a different genre:

Amazon Best Sellers Rank: #3,704 in Books

#2 in Books > Religion & Spirituality > Hinduism > **Chakras**

#9 in Books > Health, Fitness & Dieting > **Reference**

#16 in Books > Health, Fitness & Dieting > Exercise & Fitness > **Yoga**

Note that like the example above, this book is likely selling 15 to 20 copies per week, yet it's enough to place it at #2 in the Chakras category, a more obscure sub-category with less competition.

This is a good reminder to make sure your book is listed in the right sub-categories. When you or your publisher submits your book to Amazon, you usually get to pick three categories. Amazon may also assign additional categories for your book. When you maintain steady sales, you can keep your ranking lower (under 100k is a good goal) and keep your book visible in its sub-categories.

By the way, rankings for Kindle books are similar, though there isn't as much competition there so it's easier to achieve a higher ranking for your book in its Kindle sub-category.

How Amazon Cross-Promotes Books

Amazon has several features that help to cross-promote books and encourage buyers:

Frequently Bought Together – Once your book has some sales history, Amazon will likely pair it up with another book and offer it under the Frequently Bought Together feature on your book's sales page. Amazon determines what book goes here based on its own algorithms and the purchase habits of those who bought your book.

Customers Who Bought This Item Also Bought – Here you will likely see several dozen books listed, which again reveal the buying habits of your readers. If another author's book shows up under this section on your page, your book is likely to be featured under this section on their page, too.

Books on Related Topics – Some, though not all, books on Amazon have a section that lists Books on Related Topics. Amazon chooses these titles by looking at statistically improbably phrases within the books. The more often the same phrases appear in both books, the more likely they will be paired together.

What Items Do Customers Buy After Viewing This Item? Here you will find a few selections of similar books, or books that are likely your biggest competition.

This can all be useful information. You may want to get to know some of the authors recommended in these sections and find ways to work together. It can be beneficial for both of you to promote each other's work.

By the way, Amazon also sends periodic email recommendations out to its buyers who subscribe to updates from Amazon. For example, if your book is about quantum physics, there is a chance, albeit slim, that Amazon will send an email out to buyers of other quantum physics books and let them know about yours. This feature is more commonly used with buyers who have a history with the author, which means as you publish subsequent books, your past buyers may get notified. When my last book came out (*Own Your Niche*), I heard from several readers who let me know they received an email notification about the book from Amazon.

Search Inside the Book Program

Amazon allows shoppers to preview the contents of a book by serving up pages within the book, which is intended to recreate the experience of browsers in a bookstore thumbing through the pages of a book. This feature can entice readers to make a purchase decision, and if your book is done well, it should enhance sales.

This feature has been known to make some authors skittish. I have had numerous conversations with authors who did not want to make the contents of their books available for browsing. There really isn't anything to fear here. Amazon doesn't allow viewers to print your pages or download files. Viewers should not be able to see ALL pages from your book, only a select number of pages chosen by Amazon. It is unlikely that anyone could read your book from beginning to end here.

Legend has it that participation in this program also improves the chances of your book being found based on keyword searches from the text. To participate, you will need to create a Seller Central account (http://seller-central.amazon.com/) and follow the instructions to submit your book. You will submit the interior in PDF format, and can also submit the front and back covers from your book, and even an image of the spine if you so choose, though the book interior is the most important part. It should take just a few days for approval and then browsers will be able to view the contents from your book.

Get More Reviews

Like it or not, reviews on Amazon help sell books. The vast majority of potential buyers will look at reviews to assist them in making a buying decision (I know that I do). If you don't have many reviews, it can make your book look less popular than competing books with many reviews. And if you have too many negative reviews, you will undoubtedly lose buyers. If this happens, take a step back and look objectively at the negative feedback. The occasional negative review is to be expected, but a series of them may indicate a problem. Often you will find a trend that needs to be addressed in a revised edition of your book.

The point is that all authors need to focus on generating reviews on Amazon on an ongoing basis. It is believed that reviews also help Amazon rank your book. The more reviews your book receives, the more likely Amazon will be to display your book as an option in related search results.

Following are ways to generate more book reviews on Amazon:

Start with friends who have actually READ the book – This one is tricky. You don't want to ask great Aunt Edna or your mom to write a review. It will be too hard for them to be objective, and the results will show up in the reviews. Can you imagine if Aunt Edna wrote, "Oh, Jimmy's book is just wonderful. I'm so proud of him!" Yikes! Believe me, readers will notice. But you do want to reach out to friends and family—those who have actually read the book and can give a professional opinion—and ask them to take a few moments to write a review for you.

Ask Amazon Reviewers – Look for the people who have reviewed competing titles and ask them to review your book. You may need to send them a complimentary review copy, but many reviewers on Amazon will be thrilled to be asked. When you look at book reviews on Amazon, you can click on the reviewer's name and it will take you to their personal profile on Amazon, showing you other books they've reviewed. Many will list their bio or even a website, so with a bit of effort, you can track down an email address for a reviewer and reach out.

Reach out to your email subscribers – If you maintain an e-newsletter list, and you should, ask your readers to write a review.

Ask via social media – There is nothing wrong with reaching out to your social media audience and asking for their help. A post like this should work: "Did you like XYZ book? I'd appreciate it if you'd post a review on Amazon!" Don't forget to include a link to your book's page on Amazon. Make it as easy as possible.

Give away review copies – Many authors host campaigns where they give away free books specifically for review. In exchange, if the reader likes the book, he/she should write a nice review on Amazon. You can offer up this option via any means at your disposal (email, social media, to trade associations you belong to, etc.).

Ask buyers – When you sell books through your website or at a live event, consider inserting a note inside the book asking the reader to post a review. You could print this request up on a postcard or even on a business card, or if time allows, hand-write a note to include in each copy.

Offer incentive – Last fall I reached out to my audience and offered up a bonus report to anyone who posted a review within a specified time period (several weeks). This simple campaign inspired several dozen reviews from my readers with very little effort.

Remember, sometimes all you have to do is ask. The key for most of us is to *remember* to ask!

Your Amazon Public Profile and Book Reviews

If you've ever made a purchase on Amazon, you have a public user profile on the site. To locate yours, go to the "Your Account" page on Amazon (usually found in the upper right when you view any page on Amazon) and scroll down to the "Personalization" section where you will find a link to "Your Public Profile."

Here you can input a bio, list your website, upload a photo, add a caption for your photo (which should indicate that you are an author, plus your area of expertise), and add a signature. The signature line is important because when you write a book review on Amazon, your name appears along with your signature. As an example, when I review a book on Amazon, my name appears like this:

Stephanie Chandler Author of Own Your Niche: Hype-Free Internet Marketing Tactics...

One way to increase your visibility on Amazon is to write reviews for books in the same genre as yours. Each time you do this, your name and signature appear alongside your review. We all like to read reviews for books we want to purchase, and potential buyers may see yours and then want to know more about you. They can click on your name to view your public profile or simply search for your book title. You may even hear from the author of the book. I occasionally try to reach out to people who leave reviews for my books and thank them, which is another way to show appreciation for my readers and build loyalty. At the very least, that author will know your name! We all look at reviews for our books.

You can also post video reviews for books, which is another interesting way to stand out on Amazon. When you view a book page and click on "Write a Review," you will have the option to upload a video review. These often stand out among the written reviews, so if you're comfortable on camera, this can be a fun way to get extra visibility and build your personal brand.

One note when writing reviews: make sure you write positive reviews. This strategy will certainly backfire if you go around leaving negative reviews for your competitors, or any books. There are plenty of grumpy people out there leaving negative reviews for books and you don't need to be one of them. And if you believe in karma, those negative reviews can come right back to you. If I don't like a book, I personally prefer to skip leaving a review.

KDP Select

For authors with ebooks published via the Kindle Digital Publishing (KDP) program, there is an option to participate in the controversial KDP Select program. With this program, you can make your ebook (Kindle version) available in Amazon's lending library where Amazon Prime members can borrow your ebook. In exchange, Amazon sends out checks each quarter to participating authors as a sort of reward system for lending your ebook instead of selling it.

The amount you will actually earn will be determined by Amazon, based on a quarterly fund established by Amazon to compensate authors for participating in the lending program. You will receive a percentage of the quarterly fund based on that number of times your ebook was borrowed. That means that the fees you earn will change each quarter.

With the KDP Select program, you can also opt to participate in a give-away event, where you make your ebook available for free download for a period of time (from one to five days). The point of these campaigns is to help attract new readers, and thus more buzz, for your book. Authors have reported from hundreds to thousands of downloads generated during these campaigns, though fiction authors tend to achieve a higher number of downloads than nonfiction authors. Unfortunately, Amazon does not provide you with any user information so you have no way of tracking, or contacting, the people who downloaded your book.

The biggest downside of the KDP Select program is that in order to participate, you must grant Amazon exclusive rights to distribute your ebook. That means that while you are enrolled in the KDP Select program, you cannot distribute your ebook through Smashwords, Barnes and Noble's Nook store, iBooks, Sony or any other major ebook retailers. And Amazon will first verify this detail before accepting you into the program. Amazon also tries to entice authors to participate in the KDP Select program by increasing royalty rates authors earn for ebook sales in Japan, India, and Brazil—countries where frankly, most authors aren't likely to sell many books.

With all of this in mind, it's really a personal decision whether you want to participate in this program or not. If you are struggling to generate ebook sales, especially from the non-Amazon ebook retailers, then the risk is probably minimal on your part since you won't be cutting off a major book sales artery. But if your sales are cranking on the iPad or Nook, then this program probably won't make a lot of sense for you. In chapter 8, I also provide you with an alternative solution to conduct your own ebook giveaway, without working with the Amazon KDP Select program.

Link Your Print and Kindle Editions Together

If your book is available in print and Kindle ebook formats, you can alert Amazon to connect your respective sales pages. That means that when a reader views the sales page for the paperback edition of your book, she/he will also see a box below for "Other Editions" and can easily click through to the Kindle edition (and from the Kindle edition page, she/he will see the trade paperback option). Here's how:

- Go to http://kdp.amazon.com.
- Click on "Contact Us" at the footer of the page.
- Click on "Product Page," then "Linking Print" and "Kindle Editions."
- Fill in the requested information: ASIN for the Kindle version and ISBN for the print edition. Once submitted, you should see your pages linked together within a few days.

How to Give Away Copies of Your Kindle Ebook

Amazon has a feature called "Give as a Gift," which you can use to send someone a Kindle book via email. For authors, this can be quite handy for book promotion purposes. If you can drive more sales to your Kindle edition by getting others to give it as a gift, the rank for your book's sales page will improve and will ultimately lead to more visibility on Amazon, thus increasing your overall sales.

For example, let's say you agree to speak at an event or conference and then ask the event host if they would be willing to give attendees a copy of your book in Kindle format. They agree to give a copy to all 100 attendees. The host would then go to Amazon and use the Give as a Gift feature, which will allow them to email a redemption code to each attendee, one at a time. Their attendees get a bonus, while you gain new readers, increase your sales, and improve your overall sales rank on Amazon!

Incidentally, for printed books, you can also use a feature called "eGift this Item," which will send a gift card via email to the recipient and suggest that they purchase the book. However, if you want to gift copies of your printed book through Amazon, a better option is simply to purchase the book and ship it to the recipient directly.

Author Interview

Name: Allen Fahden

Website: http://funisgood.net

Books:

- *Innovation on Demand*
- *How to Be a Successful Criminal*
- *Is Half the World Crazy?*
- *The One Minute Millionaire (4 chapters)*
- *Another Boring, Derivative, Piece of Crap Business Book*

Are you traditionally published or self-published, and why did you make that choice?

Self-published. No publisher got my approach to innovation and creativity. It was too far out for the time.

Tell us a bit about your most recent book:

It's the first business book that's funny. It's called *Another Boring, Derivative, Piece of Crap Business Book*.

THE CONTENT: Its purpose is to get people working IN their strengths ON projects they're passionate about. For 150 years people have had to change themselves to fit the work. Now it's time to reverse that and change the work to fit the strengths of the people.

THE STYLE: Each chapter starts with a story about a funny promotion or misadventure that you'd think would be a disaster, but always turned out well. (Mike Veeck: Bat night with Tonya Harding; Allen Fahden: Arthur Anderson Appreciation Night during the Enron scandal.)

THE STRUCTURE: Laugh, learn, leap. This overlays with the best of training protocols that call for engagement, interesting content and application. Why laugh? A University of Maryland study shows that laughter gets more oxygen to your brain. This sets you up to learn new insights, which can then inspire new action.

Who is your target audience of readers?

Leaders who want to change their culture so they can attract and keep talent, and get the highest performance out of the talent they have. Employees who want to have more fun while contributing more.

What has been the single most effective marketing strategy you have used for promoting your book?

Through self-effacing humor, being different enough for the people and the media to notice. It saves a lot of work trying to interest people in something that's not interesting.

What are some other marketing tactics that have or haven't worked for you?

Redefining the usual ways of buying books has worked very well. I featured my first book, *Innovation on Demand*, in a one-book bookstore called ReadDundant. This got me in front of 50 million people with media coverage from *ABC-TV*, *National Public Radio*, the *BBC*, *People Magazine* and major newspapers. I plan to reopen for the new book, with a special twist: The first bricks and mortar ebook store.

How has social media impacted your success? Which social media networks do you feel generate the best results for you?

Because we have a business audience with a lot of training and consulting follow up, we plan on using LinkedIn and LinkedIn groups along with guest articles in selected business blogs.

What have been some of the biggest benefits of publishing a book?

No CEO ever spent four hours on a plane reading your business card. A book builds instant credibility for your business, allows people who don't know you to become fans, leads the way to other products, speaking, trainings and consulting.

What advice would you offer to new authors who are getting ready to promote their books?

Be different, different, different. Write the right book in the first place. Do something unique and entertaining enough and people, including the media, will want to find you.

If you were starting over today, is there anything you would do differently?

Yes. I wouldn't start over.

PART
THREE:

After the Book
is Released

Chapter 7:
Offline Marketing Tactics

"I've missed more than 9000 shots in my career. I've lost almost 300 games. 26 times, I've been trusted to take the game winning shot and missed. I've failed over and over and over again in my life. And that is why I succeed."
– Michael Jordan

THOUGH I AM AN ADVOCATE of marketing online as much as possible, there are still many tasks that you can accomplish offline.

Book Awards Programs

There are a good number of book awards programs out there where authors can compete to win an award. Most awards programs charge a fee ranging from $35 to $100 per entry, and the guidelines typically allow for books published in the previous calendar year. Some programs are extra-friendly to independent authors, and there are other programs that don't even allow indie authors to participate (they clearly haven't caught up with the times yet).

It can definitely be worthwhile to participate as long as the awards program is reputable. When your book receives an award, your title instantly changes to "award-winning author." Your book will likely get some added publicity from the awards program itself, and you can get a lot of promotional mileage from winning a single award.

Many programs provide stickers you can place on your books to promote your winning status, and badges you can feature on your website. You can also update your book's sales pages and descriptions in online bookstores to acknowledge the award. Your award-winning author status can impress prospective readers and boost sales. And perhaps even more importantly, winning an award can bring a tremendous amount of personal satisfaction. It's a big accomplishment to write a book in the first place, and to have your work recognized can be quite rewarding.

Following are some top book awards programs for authors.

Ben Franklin Book Awards
Recognizes independently published books.
http://ibpabenjaminfranklinawards.com/

Global Ebook Awards
The first awards program exclusively for ebooks, hosted by self-publishing godfather Dan Poynter.
http://globalebookawards.com/

Foreword Book of the Year
Hosted by *Foreword* magazine, this is an indie-friendly awards program.
https://www.forewordreviews.com/services/book-awards/botya/

Nautilus Book Awards
Recognizes books that promote spiritual growth, conscious living, and positive social change.
http://www.nautilusbookawards.com/

National Indie Excellence Book Awards
Many categories to choose from and honors independently published titles.
http://www.indieexcellence.com/

The Eric Hoffer Awards
Recognizes excellence in independently produced books.
http://www.hofferaward.com/

Small Business Book Awards
No fee to enter, and awards are given based on peer voting.
http:// bookawards.smallbiztrends.com/

Give Away Copies

The goal with your book is to get people talking about it and build buzz. One way to accomplish this is to give books away. You should allow for this into your marketing plan and budget. Make sure to set aside dozens of books to give away for promotional purposes.

Give your books freely to reporters, reviewers, bloggers, and anyone else who may be influential in helping you reach your target audience. Keep shipping envelopes on hand so you can easily send out copies. Always include a personal note with any copy you send out, and don't be afraid to follow up via email.

I receive several dozen books from authors each year, which I find odd since I don't write book reviews. However, those authors are likely hoping that I will notice their books and perhaps mention them in some way. This is not a bad strategy, though a better focus is to send books to people who actually review books, or to people you know.

You can also give away books at events, such as your local Chamber of Commerce monthly luncheon. If they raffle off door prizes, provide a copy. Some authors even leave copies in lobbies and waiting rooms at doctor's offices, car washes, coffee shops, and other locations. I'm not convinced this will lead to explosive sales, but it is an option.

AUTHOR TIP: Even if you route most of your book sales to Amazon, you will need a convenient way to ship out copies to media people and professional contacts. Media mail is an inexpensive shipping option provided by the USPS, though it can take more time to reach its recipient. A better option is Priority Mail. The USPS offers flat rate shipping envelopes that current cost around $5 to ship. You can get the envelopes free of charge from your local post office or by ordering online at http://usps.com. You can also print postage directly from the USPS website. If you do a lot of shipping, you may also enjoy the convenience of printing postage with http://stamps.com.

Book Signing Events

New authors often ask me about book signing events. They want to know how to get them set up and what to do. My advice? They are rarely worth your time.

While it may sound exciting to sit at a table in Barnes and Noble and enjoy a line of customers eager to purchase your book, that's not how it usually goes down. A long time ago I read somewhere that the average number of books sold at a book signing is eight copies. As a former bookstore owner, I can confirm that is about right (unless your last name is Grisham or Rowling).

Consider what is involved. You have to first take time to try to book the appearance, which means trekking down to your local bookstore and talking to the manager. Time spent = 1 hour.

Then you have to show up prepared, which means bringing along some items for your signing table. Maybe some bookmarks, handouts, a bowl of candy, some flowers, etc. So you arrive early to set up, then park it there for three hours, wrap up and return home. Total time spent = 5 hours, bringing you to a grand total of six hours to sell an average of eight books! At that rate you're not even earning minimum wage.

Back when I owned a bookstore, we held author events every weekend. The vast majority of authors sold eight books or less. I remember one author who didn't sell a single book and many who sold less than five. Ouch.

The authors who sold more than eight books typically invited friends and family. They had mailing lists, alumni groups, coworkers, and other networks that showed up to give support. Once in awhile, coverage in the local paper or news program would stir up some shoppers, but even those mentions fell flat more often than not.

I was once part of a big book launch event for one of the *Chicken Soup for the Soul* books. There were three of us local contributors, including one with some local celebrity appeal. We received coverage on the morning TV news and radio, and Barnes and Noble positioned our table directly at the front door. It was a busy Saturday morning and we even had trays of free chocolate-covered strawberries on our table. We had all the makings for a stellar signing event. Those strawberries went like crazy! We were there for three hours and had plenty of shoppers stop by to chat and have a treat. Guess how many books we sold? Twelve. Hey, at least we beat the average!

Here's a better option: conduct an event. Show up as a speaker, engage your audience, and you'll sell plenty of books. Also an exception to the rule: your book launch party. When you promote the release of your book to friends, colleagues, and family, you're going to make some sales.

So instead of sitting alone at a table waiting for customers to wander by and feeling like a peddler, find more productive ways to generate book sales. Speak at local service groups and trade associations. Collaborate with other authors to hold a seminar. Host a contest, support a charity, or finally start using social media! Just save yourself the trouble of doing book signing events.

How to Find Book Reviewers

Most book reviews in major publications focus on fiction so it's harder to find sources willing to review nonfiction. However, here's a little trick that has worked for me:

Create a Google Alert with the keywords "book review" + <genre>. So yours might be *"book review" memoir* or *"book review" health*. Note that "book review" is in quotes to ensure the exact phrase is found.

You will begin receiving alerts with links to book reviews on news sites and blogs. Then, view the review links, verify that the site is credible and generates some decent traffic, and make note of the reporter. And of course this strategy will work with a basic Google search as well, though an Alert will keep you informed of current book review listings.

Once you locate reviews, look for editorial contact information so that you can reach out to the reporter directly or the editor who covers the appropriate news section. Send a note asking if they would like a review copy of your book along with a brief overview of what it is about.

By the way, major magazines want to review books months in advance of the book's release, and most newspapers will want to review the book as soon as it is available.

Write for Print Publications

Publishing articles in newspapers, trade newsletters and magazines can be an excellent way to attract a new audience of book readers. Many publications will print your article along with your bio and website link.

Trade magazines and neighborhood newspapers are an excellent place to start since they are often in need of writers. Consumer magazines can also be a source for your articles, although the popular magazines that you find on the checkout stands of grocery stores are the most difficult to break in to. It is best to start with smaller or regional publications.

I have personally had tremendous success over the years by submitting my articles to various trade association newsletters, smaller business magazines, and newspapers. In most cases you won't even know the article was printed because you've already granted permission and editors are too busy to follow up. You will only know the article ran if you happen to see it yourself or hear from a reader—or notice a nice spike in book sales!

To get started, visit your local bookstore to find smaller magazines or conduct searches on Google. You can also search sites like www.newspapers.com, or http://newsdirectory.com. Locate contact information for the editor in the publication masthead or website. Many websites offer writer's guidelines where the editor will indicate whether she/he accepts submissions via email and what kinds of articles the publication accepts. The most important item to note here is that you are submitting an article for *reprint—something you've published elsewhere (like on your blog)*. The larger publications rarely accept reprints and in the journalism world, this is an important distinction.

Incidentally, submitting articles to these publications can also lead to article assignments. Many times after submitting articles, I have been contacted by the editor and assigned a story. And if you're assigned to write a story, you get paid. You won't retire off of the funds you earn from writing for smaller publications, but consider it a bonus to get paid to promote yourself!

Use the following format to submit your articles via email. Be sure to simply paste the article content into the body of the email since editors may not be willing to open attachments.

> Resumes That Rock
> By Edna Entrepreneur
> Word count: 975
> <insert article body>
> <insert author bio>
> *This article may be reprinted provided the author bio is included.
> Thank you very much for your consideration.
> Edna Entrepreneur
> <insert contact information>

Run a Group with Meetup.com

In 2006, I stumbled upon what I have come to call a happy accident. I wanted to network with fellow speakers in my area so I decided to launch a group called The Sacramento Speakers Network, which I organized through Meetup.com, a social site for organizing local events. The first meeting was held with four people at a local Starbucks, and today we have over 1,000 members and average 50 to 60 attendees at the monthly meeting.

Meetup.com is a powerful tool for organizing groups and events. In any given city you can find a wide variety of options from business-related groups, singles groups, hiking clubs, religious organizations, book clubs and much, much more. The site makes it easy to host and manage a local group, and also cross-promotes groups, helping site visitors find other interests.

I never envisioned the speakers' network getting so big. I started the group simply because I wanted to network with other speakers in the area and see how we could support each other—and I didn't realize that we would fill such a great need in the community. We are the largest business-related Meetup group in the Sacramento area and I'm often asked how we have built such a big membership base. Here's what makes this group work:

1. **Meeting Focus** - We are not a Toastmasters group and don't practice speaking, nor do we have the strict membership requirements of the National Speakers Association. Instead we focus on *the business of speaking*. This is a unique niche focus that isn't available anywhere else in the region.

2. **Meeting Format** - Every member gets a 30-second introduction, which serves as a promotion tool for attendees as well as a way for the entire group to get to know each other. It's interesting and fun (thanks to a lot of humor in the room) and sets the tone for the meeting.

3. **Relevant Guest Speakers** - I bring in a guest speaker every month. Speakers cover topics related to speaking and business. We've had a literary agent, professional keynoters who have shared insights on the industry, book writing coaches, web technology discussions and more.

4. **The Group Mastermind** - One thing that makes our group unique

is our mastermind session. During the final 15 minutes of the meeting, we draw business cards. When a card is drawn, the member gets five minutes to share a business issue or challenge and get positive, supportive feedback from the group. For example, at a recent meeting one of our members wanted suggestions for how he should prepare before a speaking engagement. He received feedback from the group about how to research his audience, prepare hand-outs and make his presentation memorable. These exchanges end up being helpful and interesting to everyone in the room.

5. **Door Prizes!** - Because our group attracts a lot of authors and coaches, we have a hearty raffle for door prizes at the end of the meeting. Members donate books, videos, CDs, workbooks, gift certificates and more. We draw business cards and winners come up to pick a prize. This is a lot of fun for all.

6. **Word of Mouth** - I have never advertised this group. It's not on my business card and it's admittedly not something I spend time promoting. The members are loyal and tell their friends. It's not uncommon for a new attendee to tell me that three different people told her about the group and she finally decided to check us out.

7. **Really Smart People** - What we have collectively done is create a fun and productive experience for attendees. At any given meeting our attendees can include veterinarians, CPAs, life and business coaches, doctors, chiropractors, psychologists, attorneys, health coaches, financial advisors, authors… and the list goes on. Because our focus is unique, it attracts a really smart group of people, and the word of mouth continues to help the group expand.

8. **Consistency** - We meet the first Wednesday night each month and have since the beginning. The meeting date and time is predictable. The biggest challenge has been finding venues since we have outgrown many locations. We used to meet in restaurants but because the group has gotten so large, we now rent meeting space at a local hotel. This serves as a central location with a professional atmosphere and fits the needs of our group very well.

9. **Money Matters** - Because of the size of the group and its focus, we've had several corporate sponsors over the years. This is a nice perk that provides added funding for the group. We also charge a

meeting fee to cover room rental and other costs, and provide the guest speaker with a gift card.

10. **Group Organization** - Though I lead the group, I do have volunteers that help coordinate details, collect payments at the door, greet members, etc. While it may sound like a lot of work to coordinate a large group like this, it really isn't. I book speakers several months in advance and by meeting at the same venue at the same time each month, there aren't many other details to manage. It's pretty darn easy!

I will add that a good 80% of my business comes from the Internet and online relationships. And because of this, I really don't have to get out in my community and network. However, being an entrepreneur can be isolating. I love getting out and connecting with other entrepreneurs. We share a common bond and it's fun to get that in-person interaction that is absent from most of my workdays.

I call this group a happy accident because it has grown so large, it's still going strong years later, and it has helped me personally get known in my community. I have acquired many clients from the group, and have also booked many speaking engagements as a result.

So if you want to get known in your own backyard, I highly recommend launching your own niche group via Meetup.com. It's a powerful tool for locating people in your community and managing the details for your monthly events calendar. It's also a great place to locate groups that may be of interest to you as an attendee.

Direct Mail Campaigns

One of the most traditional forms of marketing is with direct mail, which involves sending out sales letters, postcards, newsletters, flyers, and other marketing collateral via good old U.S. mail. Because our world has become so Internet-centric, I think a lot of people have forgotten about this strategy, which can still be quite effective if done correctly.

Of all the direct mail options, postcards remain my favorite type of marketing collateral for a bunch of reasons. For starters, they are relatively inexpensive to print and mail. Also, since less than 5% of direct mail is actually opened by recipients, postcards greatly increase your chances of getting people to notice because they stand out in a sea of envelopes. I also favor over-sized postcards (8.5 x 5.5) because these *really* stand out.

Here are some of the ways to use postcards for marketing:

Individual Products and Services - When I launch a new product or service, I usually have a postcard designed. I either rent a mailing list (from a source like http://InfoUSA.com) or send them out to my internal mailing list of readers and clients.

Package Inserts - Postcards make great inserts in packages that are mailed out. I like to write a personal note on the back of a postcard when sending something along to a client or a prospect.

Conferences and Events - Postcards also work well on display tables at conferences and events. They are more substantial than a flier and usually have more aesthetic appeal (especially the over-sized version).

Bag Stuffers - When I was invited to submit 500 flyers for stuffing in conference swag bags, I decided to use postcards instead. In lieu of a purely promotional postcard, I printed up a list of tips for the audience on the front of the card and saved the promotional messaging for the back of the card. My goal was to provide something that attendees would keep or even post next to their desks.

Personal Stationary - There are plenty of places to buy standard business stationary, but for years I have used custom postcards instead of boring note cards. I purchase high-quality photo art from http://istockphoto.com and place a favorite motivational quote across the image. On the back side, I simply include my contact information at the bottom and leave plenty of room for writing a note. Though I love technology and use it well every day, I still cherish a hand-written note and try to write them as often as possible.

Live Event Promotion - Recently, a professional speaker shared a story about how she used direct mail postcards to fill a workshop that she held several years ago. She rented a targeted mailing list for her audience of dentists, set a registration fee of $199, and packed the house.

Book Promotion - Direct mail campaigns can be effective for selling books if you're careful not to blow your budget. An author of a history book told me that he sends postcards to librarians to promote his books, and as a result has sold over 1,000 copies. You could also create postcards to offer review copies of your book to targeted prospects, such as professors at universities. Because it's so hard to justify spending big bucks to market books alone, make sure to do a small test mailing and monitor the results you get. If you send out 100 postcards and only sell two books, you will need to rethink your strategy. But if you mail out 100 postcards and get an order for 1,000 books as a result, then clearly the strategy you're using is working!

Author Interview

Your Name: Steve Sisgold

Website: http://OneDream.com

Books:

- *What's Your Body Telling You?*

Are you traditionally published or self-published, and why did you make that choice?

I chose going the publisher route and signed with McGraw-Hill over some other publisher's offer, because I liked their team of savvy New York women and the ideas they had for my book, from the cover to accepting all of my stories and processes. They offered me a hardcover and an earlier release date and I also sensed that McGraw-Hill as my publisher would add credibility for my work (Whole Body Intelligence or WBI), propel my speaking and coaching career, and get me on radio and TV—and it did exactly that. I also wanted some media and marketing support that they offered me.

I also coach people who want 100% control of their book, from editing to royalties and don't want to wait 18 months to get their book out, so I advise them to self-publish. Today, there are so many options to self-publish and have professional support too. The main thing is to be honest with yourself on how you can get your book out there: an ebook, self-published or go sell someone on your idea to front the expense and print it for you.

Tell us a bit about your most recent book:

I spent the past 25 years studying and teaching the relationship between beliefs held in the body and success, how the body "billboard" sends micro messages that affect authentic communication and how self-awareness lowers stress and boosts peak performance. As Einstein said, "You can't solve a problem with the same thinking that created it," so I found the fastest way to help clients was to look at another intelligence; what I call BQ; accessing from your instincts, and your whole body full of memories and information. I asked the question, "What's your body telling you right now?" (Hence the title of my book!) at least 10,000 times in sessions, seminars and talks across the country, and saw thousands of people learn to navigate successfully through life's challenges using proven whole body techniques for concentrated focus and confidence, and discern truth from fear and avoid dangerous impulsive reactions.

As you read *What's Your Body Telling You?* you identify, release and change the subconscious beliefs that sabotage your happiness and success. You learn to shift from confusion to clarity in an instant, becoming proactive and inspired in making important life decisions, and learn to communicate with far greater effectiveness and clarity in both your personal and professional lives.

WYBTY? is filled with many inspirational tales including how I used WBI to become the # 1 sales producer in a major corporation, followed my own body's instincts all the way to India and had miraculous gifts come my way, and even when I went into the darkest corners of Poland and Germany, where I was joined by my colleague and friend Gay Hendricks, and had one of the greatest healings of my life.

Who is your target audience of readers?

People who want to learn more about self-awareness and are motivated to change patterns and habits that sabotage their happiness. That can range from someone wanting to improve their health, relationships, career and wants a new approach.

Body oriented professionals of all kinds enjoy learning new approaches to use in their own practice, which inspired me to train others in WBI which I am enjoying doing. People going through transitions and who are seeking a sense of purpose are drawn to my book as well. My demographic is broad because everyone has a body and wants to know how to use it to access information for improving every area of life, which is what my book does.

What has been the single most effective marketing strategy you have used for promoting your book?

Single most is tough to pinpoint. Highlights for me were media wins like a *PBS* interview or an in person interview with Dr. Laura Berman on the Oprah Network. My book launch where friends mailed to their lists was a big boost. Bookstore signings got me on the *San Francisco Chronicle* and Amazon Best Sellers lists.

What are some other marketing tactics that have or haven't worked for you?

Most small blog radio shows didn't have many listeners but like most excited to be interviewed authors I had to go through several to realize that. Some teleconferences where all guest experts mail out the promotion worked very well in attracting new people to my community. Some publicists got me results and some got paid very well for no results. I learned that either me or someone else has to follow up. Mailing packages and hoping people will call doesn't do it. Also I spoke at some events where I sold a lot of books and some very little, depending on the audience.

I also have gotten bumps in book sales or business for blogging for Psychology Today and other sites.

How has social media impacted your success? Which social media networks do you feel generate the best results for you?

I have seen some direct results from exposure through Facebook posts, tweets that offer tips and some email promotional campaigns. I have used YouTube videos successfully also to attract people to my website or to go buy my book or audio series.

What have been some of the biggest benefits of publishing a book?

All of the above.

I carried wisdom and experience in my brain for a long time so I wanted to get it out and on paper. I also wanted as I stated above, a boost in my career, which it has. From media to paid speaking events, it was my book that drew them to me or gave me the "expert" title, which they wanted.

What advice would you offer to new authors who are getting ready to promote their books?

Learn from others who have been through the process, even if you have to pay them for coaching. I paid people to teach me how to do many aspects of writing, marketing and producing other products to help book sales too. I still made some mistakes and extra expenditures I now advise people not to make, so each of us learn and there's no reason to go it alone.

If you were starting over today, is there anything you would do differently?

I would spend less time on just about any radio show, as I am more selective now with my time, plus I would book even more speaking events, paid or free just to get in front of people, and I would research more and spend less on some of the marketing and publicity programs I bought into and got very little from. Many author friends of mine on their second and third books don't use the book launch companies or book promo experts, as they now know what to do and you can find someone to teach you to do it or hire an administrative person to do it for a lot less.

Is there anything else you would like to add?

Breathe in and embody your book idea, then breathe out and start writing. There are great editors out there so just get your ideas out on paper or tape and that builds momentum. There are also writer's conferences and books on how to write a book proposal or market your book. Learn about the industry, walk through bookstores and libraries and see what books speak out to you and what formats appeal to you. It will help you embrace the idea of being an author. Oh yeah, and trust your gut and heart the most. Enjoy the journey.

Chapter 8:
Online Marketing Tactics

"Creativity makes a leap, then looks to see where it is."
– Mason Cooley

MARKETING MY BOOKS and my personal brand online has had a tremendous impact on my career as an author. Even if you're not tech savvy, you can still learn how to promote your books and find opportunities online. It's not as difficult as you might think!

Host Your Own Ebook Giveaway (Without Amazon KDP)

In late 2012, I decided to host a free ebook promotion where I gave away copies of my latest book, *Own Your Niche*, free of charge for three days. My goal was to give away 400 copies in three days. Over 72 hours, I was surprised to tally up over 1,000 registrations from users who downloaded the book, which far exceeded my expectations.

There has been a lot of buzz recently about ebook promotions, specifically with Amazon's KDP Select program, which allows you to give your book away to Kindle users for up to five days. I chose not to participate in Amazon's program primarily because Amazon requires exclusive distribution rights, which meant that I would have to cut off my distribution via Smashwords, which would prevent my ebook from being available for Nook readers, iPad users, etc. The other downside of promoting with Amazon is that you never know who downloaded your ebook. There is no email address capture or any way for the author to communicate with readers after the promotion is over.

So, I decided to launch my own campaign. Here's how it all went down:

1. I set up a registration page on my site where visitors could fill out a form with their first name, last name, and email address. Short

and sweet. My web designer created the form, which put all email addresses into a database that I could export and then import into my email marketing system.

2. After registering, users received an email with a link to a page to download the ebook. I offered it in two formats: PDF or Smashwords. For PDF, they simply had to save the link to their computer. If they chose Smashwords, they had to go through the steps of purchasing the book with a free discount code.

3. I offered up an extra bonus for readers, letting them know that if they wrote a review in the next 30 days and posted it on Amazon, BN.com, Smashwords, their own blogs or social media sites, and then sent me a link to confirm, I would send them an additional nine bonus download items (reports, worksheets, etc.). Within the first day of this offer, I generated twelve sparkling new reviews.

Ebook Giveaway Promotion Strategy

To generate buzz for this promotion, I did the following:

1. Announced via my social media networks each day with messages like, "Just two days left to grab your free ebook: Own Your Niche! <link>"

2. Added a Tweet button to the registration page so that users could easily tweet out a pre-written message: "Free Internet Marketing Book: Own Your Niche by Stephanie Chandler @bizauthor Grab your copy here: <link>". Tweets were a big part of this campaign with tens of thousands of Twitter users reached.

3. Sent an email announcement to each of my mailing lists (I have several), letting subscribers know I wouldn't be reminding them again so they shouldn't wait to download the book. (I'm not a big fan of email blasts so I wasn't going to bug my subscribers more than once, though many marketers would disagree with this approach and would suggest a reminder on the last day. I'm sure if I had done that, there would have been an additional flurry of downloads.)

What I Would Do Differently Next Time

There were a few glitches with my process and the download page. I was in a hurry to launch and didn't test the process thoroughly. Next time, I would definitely test the process two or three times to make sure the links are delivered as expected and everything is in working order.

I didn't reach out to any of my peers or alliance partners to ask for their support, though several spotted the promotion and mentioned it on their own to their various social networks. However, next time I will make a point to let others know about the campaign and simply ask them to help spread the word.

It would have been interesting to send out a press release via PRWeb for this campaign to see if it got mentioned by any bloggers. At the very least, press releases on PRWeb can drive traffic so that can be a helpful strategy.

Why I Gave My Ebook Away

If you're wondering why the heck I'd be thrilled about giving away over 1,000 copies of my ebook, let me fill you in. The goal for every author should be to get your book into the hands of as many readers as possible, and giving them away is an easy way to do that. Even if just 10% of those who downloaded the book tell a friend about it, that will create some ongoing buzz and interest in the book.

Offering the additional bonus items also helped to spur some great online reviews. And because I hosted this giveaway myself, all who registered were added to my mailing list. My book also ties in nicely with my business, so the campaign helped me expand my reach with potential clients as well.

It doesn't cost anything to give away a digital book and I'd run a campaign like this again in a heartbeat. It was great fun to hear back from gracious readers, thanking me for my generosity and complimenting the book. You can't ask for more than that!

Most importantly, I absolutely did not view this as revenue lost—it was quite the opposite. Hundreds of people read my book who may not have even heard about it before all those tweets were unleashed on Twitter. In the months that followed, book sales spiked substantially. I can only attribute that to word of mouth since I didn't land any major media coverage during that time, nor was I running any other campaigns. The upside was far greater than the downside.

So if you're looking for a way to stir up some interest for your book, a free giveaway campaign can work really well. It's relatively easy to execute, just make sure you plan ahead and put the right processes in place. Also, note that I've been building my audience for YEARS. I am quite active with social media, and have mailing lists of subscribers who have been with me for a long time, so I have built a lot of loyalty over time. But even without a large network, you can certainly build plenty of buzz and add new subscribers to your mailing list—and that alone can be golden.

Participate in Blog Carnivals

A blog carnival is a blog post that features a round-up of interesting blog posts from other websites. For example, a weight loss blog might feature a round-up of recent blog posts from various weight loss experts, personal trainers, and other industry blogs. The round-up (carnival) usually includes between 10 to 50 blog posts, including blog post title and a link for each, and sometimes a bit of commentary about what readers will learn from reading each post in the carnival.

When one of your blog posts is featured in a carnival on a popular website, it can attract some great exposure and traffic. You can use Google to search for industry blogs that run blog carnivals, or you can utilize the top blog carnival website and search for opportunities to contribute: http://blogcarnival.com/bc/alist.html.

Conversely, you can also host blog carnivals on your own blog. To do this, create a regular feature on your blog, once a week or once per month, where you list compelling industry blog posts. You can find content from the industry blogs that you follow, use Google search to find resources, and you can also allow others to submit their posts for consideration (create a submission form on your site). You can also register your carnival for free and solicit contributions via http://blogcarnival.com/bc/.

Once the carnival post is published live, notify contributors and ask them to promote the link to your carnival. If you are successful at locating the best of the best in your industry on a regular basis, you can attract lots of traffic from repeat visitors who want to discover interesting industry blog posts.

AUTHOR TIP: I'm often asked about Goodreads (http://goodreads.com) and Red Room (http://redroom.com), which are social media-type sites where authors can create accounts and interact with readers. I believe that both of these sites provide more value for fiction authors since fiction readers tend to discuss books more with each other. However, it never hurts to create additional visibility for yourself online. At the very least, create a profile on Goodreads and import your blog feed link. You may occasionally generate comments from readers there, and you can get notified of activity via email.

Write for Websites

Promoting with articles has long been one of my favorite book marketing strategies, though the rules have changed over the years due to changes with Google. You used to be able to take an article and submit it to dozens of article content directories, such as http://ezinearticles.com, and your article would be picked up for reprint by other websites, blogs, and newsletters. While this can still work to bring you some additional exposure for your work, it doesn't generate as much traffic as it used to. Google doesn't like seeing the same content on multiple websites, so it will only serve up one instance of an article in search results. For example, if you wrote an article called "How to Care for Your Chihuahua," and then submitted it to several websites, when you searched for that article on Google the article would only appear one time—most likely from either the site that featured the article first or the site with the highest Google ranking. The bottom line: Articles submitted to directories no longer generate the link juice they used to.

However, there are still some great opportunities to write content for other websites, and specifically for those that reach your target audience of readers. When you write for an industry site (an expert on vegan living could write for a health site) or a popular media site (like Huffingtonpost.com), you can build your brand with readers, spur book sales, and bring traffic back to your site, thanks to the bio that is included at the end of your post.

Here's how to get started:

1. Research and identify industry websites that reach your target audience. Ideally, you should look for popular, high-traffic sites.

2. Search for submission guidelines since many sites offer guidelines for contributing. If you can't find these, contact the content editor or site owner and send a pitch. Let him/her know that you are an authority on your subject matter and that you'd like to contribute articles to the site. Note that most sites will not pay you for content, and instead offer exposure for you through your bio on the site.

3. Understand the guidelines. Many sites will require "first rights," which mean the article you contribute cannot have been previously published elsewhere. In many cases, there is some kind of time limit—30 or 60 days—and after that you can re-publish the article on your own site or elsewhere. If the site requires "exclusive rights," that means that you cannot repurpose the article anywhere else. Typically only the very large media sites require exclusive rights, and in exchange you should be paid for those. If a small, lesser known site requests exclusive rights, consider whether or not that is worth it to you. You should have the right to repurpose your content unless you are getting paid.

4. Write really great content and article headlines. Follow any guidelines provided by the site, and be sure to include a single paragraph bio at the end that explains who you are, includes your book title, and a link to your website. As an added bonus, posting your articles online adds links pointing back to your website. This can be great for search engine optimization since Google wants to see lots of incoming links to your website.

5. Don't be afraid to pitch to the major media sites (the online version of your favorite magazine)—they need content, too! Start by asking friends and peers if they know any editorial contacts at the site since referrals always help. If that doesn't work, do some research to figure out who manages the blog content for the site, or for a certain category on the site. Then take a deep breath and send a dazzling pitch. Let the editor know about your expertise and provide a few links to view samples of your work, whether on other media sites (ideally) or on your own blog. Also, suggest some topics you'd like to write about, especially topics that are particularly timely. For example, if you want to write for a major business magazine website and you have experience with the latest social media trend, suggest that as your first article topic. You'll never know until you ask.

Promote with Podcasts

In mid-2012, Apple released an app specifically for podcasts, making it easier than ever for listeners to find podcast content on their iPhones and iPads. A podcast is a downloadable recording (MP3 format), and podcasts are typically delivered as a series. Listeners can download and listen on iPods, iPhones, and other mobile devices, or on a computer. They can also subscribe to a podcast feed to be notified when a new recording is available for download.

There are thousands of podcast programs produced today, and some have hundreds of thousands of regular listeners. Podcast programs are often conducted like radio interviews, where the host interviews one or more guests, though some podcasts are instructional with the host delivering educational content.

For business purposes, it's relatively easy to produce your own podcast program and it provides another powerful way to reach your target audience. Here's how to get started:

Podcasting Basics

- Give your podcast program an appealing title (search the iTunes store for examples).

- Be very clear about who your target audience is and what kinds of content they will be interested in.

- Visit the iTunes store and sample some podcasts to learn how they are conducted, and what you like and don't like.

- Invest in a USB headset with microphone that plugs into your computer. This should run you between $30 to $60.

Tips for Creating Great Podcast Content

- Keep it relatively informal. Listeners tend to prefer more casual podcast content.

- Make it compelling for your target audience. It's always about your target audience.

- Invite interesting guests and conduct productive conversations.

- Pay attention to which topics get the most response and produce more like them!

- Podcast length can vary. You can create short recordings with quick tips that last just a few minutes, or you can deliver hour-long programming.

Podcast Recording Options

- You can purchase a recording device to connect to your phone if conducting interviews on a land line.

- The teleconference services, such as http://instantteleseminar.com and http://freeconferencecall.com offer the ability to record conference lines.

- If you prefer to use Skype, you can get recording services via http://voipcallrecording.com/, http://www.pamela.biz/en/, or http://www.easyvoiprecorder.org/.

Podcast Editing Options

- Audacity is free and relatively easy to use: http://audacity.com.

- Garage Band is available for Mac users: http://www.apple.com/ilife/garageband/.

Podcast Publishing and Distribution Options

- Note that you should have a graphic image designed to display with your podcast content.

- Utilize a service to handle publishing and distribution. Liberated Syndication offers great and affordable options: http://libsyn.com/. This should take care of your major syndication needs.

- If you prefer the DIY approach, submit to the iTunes store directly. Details are here: http://www.apple.com/itunes/podcasts/specs.html

Don't forget to promote your podcasts to your audience. Post them to your blog and announce them via social media. Soon you could build a substantial audience!

Quora (http://quora.com) is a site where users can ask questions and experts provide answers. You can showcase your authority in your field by actively participating and answering questions for your users here. You can do the same thing over at http://allexperts.com.

Start an Internet Radio Show

A lot of authors have enjoyed building their audience by hosting their own radio shows. One of the most popular Internet radio sites is http://blogtalkradio.com, and for a small monthly subscription fee, you can utilize tools to record your programs, air them live, and make the recordings available for listeners to download.

You can also decide the interval for your programming. The most popular format is to host a weekly show, though some host a daily program and others host theirs just once or twice per month. Shows typically last 60 minutes, though you can set a time frame that works for you.

As a host, you can invite interesting guests and conduct interviews during your program. Some hosts feature several guests over the course of an hour, while others feature one guest for the entire hour. What's most important is that you come prepared, ask great questions, and create an entertaining experience for your audience. In my experience, the hosts that are most successful are the ones who know how to keep the banter going, who aren't afraid to stray from their prepared list of questions, and who also know how to make guests feel at ease.

After each interview is completed, you can archive the recording on your radio show site and you can even distribute the recording through iTunes or Liberated Syndication (http://libsyn.com). Your radio program service should also provide you with statistics, including how many listened in live, how many downloaded the recording, and how many subscribed to your RSS feed.

Aside from the benefit of building your brand by hosting a show, you can build some great alliances by getting to know your guests. As you invite influential industry experts to be guests on your program, you will naturally build alliances and rapport. You never know where those connections may lead. Also, don't forget to ask your guests to help promote their appearance on your show both before and after the interview is conducted.

Host Webinars and Teleseminars

By now you're probably familiar with webinars and teleseminars. A webinar is an event conducted on a computer, which typically shows slides or a visual demonstration to attendees. A teleseminar is conducted by phone, where participants dial in to a conference line and listen to the host either present some kind of material or interview a guest (similar to a radio show).

There are two primary ways to benefit from hosting these types of events. First, when you host them for free, you can require registration and collect email addresses from attendees. This can be an effective way to build a mailing list and a following at the same time. You can also charge for access to your events.

Some authors host teleseminars or webinars on a monthly or weekly basis, while others host them periodically when they have something new to promote. You are not bound by any schedule and can decide for yourself how often you want to host these. But with each new event that you host, you create something new to promote to your audience and beyond, with one of the goals being to entice new attendees to participate and introduce them to what you do. For many coaches and consultants, hosting regular events is a primary way they attract new clients.

You can also go beyond the one-time event, and conduct a series or a class. Over the years I have used the teleseminar format to teach courses that lasted from three to six weeks (one event per week). When I conduct training courses like this, I give a lecture and assign homework to participants. They also receive the recording after the event. These events become a revenue stream, and participants pay from $99 to $299 depending on the content. Once a course is completed, it also becomes a product you can later sell in digital download format.

You can also use either the teleseminar or webinar formats to host an entire online conference. Since 2010, I have hosted the Nonfiction Writers Conference (http://nonfictionwritersconference.com), a virtual event conducted via teleseminar with 15 speakers over three days. Participants purchase access to the conference and can attend from anywhere in the world. If your industry doesn't yet have an online conference, why not start your own?

Tools for Hosting Webinars and Teleseminars

- ▦ Go To Meeting, for webinars: http://gotomeeting.com

- ▦ Instant Teleseminar, for teleseminars and webinars (my favorite choice): http://instantteleseminar.com

- ▦ Free Conference, for teleseminars: http://freeconference.com

AUTHOR TIP: One excellent tool for managing online event registration is Eventbrite (http://eventbrite.com). There is no fee for using it to manage free events, and you'll pay a nominal fee per registration for paid events (or you can pass the fee along to your buyers). This tool gives you a widget to promote registration on your website, makes it easy to communicate with attendees, and you can download a spreadsheet with attendee contact information.

Online Contests

A fun way to generate some buzz online is to host a contest, and there are many ways to accomplish this. Here are some ideas:

Comment Contest – Give something away via your blog by asking participants to post a comment. I once worked with Dell to give away a printer through my website by asking my blog readers to share their best productivity tip in the comments. The contest generated a lot of buzz both via social media sharing (people letting their networks know about the contest), and through traffic to the site. We let the contest run for a week and then chose a winner at random.

Retweet Contest – If you're a Twitter user, you can host a contest that people can enter by retweeting something you specify. For example, you might decide to give away a copy of your book each day for 10 days. First, you would need to create a page on your website that describes the rules of the contest, and then you would need to craft a tweet like this: *"Win a copy of "Extreme Skincare Solutions" by @bizauthor, RT to enter! #freeskincarebook <link to contest rules>."*

Note that your promotional tweet must be short enough to allow participants to retweet it (120 characters or less). You will also need a way to track those retweets, by monitoring the hashtag or mentions of your Twitter handle. You can also use a Twitter contest app such as http://www.binkd.com/free-twitter-contest-app/ or http://interactwive.com/.

Photo or Video Contest – You can ask your audience to participate in a more interactive contest by sharing photos or videos. For example, you might ask your readers to share photos of themselves reading your book. For videos, you could ask your audience to submit their funniest dance moves or explain reasons why they are most in need of a consultation with you.

Contests like these require some extra effort since you'll have to provide a place—and a way—for your audience to share their photos or videos. You could create a form on your website where they can submit them, or you could use a contest app such as http://www.binkd.com/photo-contest-app/, http://corp.wishpond.com/photo-contest/, http://woobox.com/photocontests, http://pages.launchpad6.com/, or http://www.strutta.com.

Vote Contests – If you want to engage your community, get them to vote for something. For example, Anita Campbell and her team at http://smallbiztrends.com host an annual Small Business Influencers contest. There is a nomination period that lasts several weeks, where anyone can nominate someone they feel is influential in the small business community. Then, the voting period opens up and the audience is unleashed! Those who are nominated typically promote the contest to their audiences several times, asking for their support. After the voting period ends, the top ten influencers based on votes are honored in each category, plus a team of judges also chooses an overall Top 100 Small Business Influencers, and they are honored at an annual awards event in New York (I was thrilled to receive this award in 2012!). Voting contests can create a lot of social media buzz and phenomenal website traffic.

You will need to leverage either custom software or an app to manage a contest like this. One option is available here: http://corp.wishpond.com/vote-contest/.

Facebook Contests – Many big company brands leverage contests on Facebook to encourage new page Likes and to get their audience engaged. You can use any of the previously mentioned contest strategies on Facebook, or conduct sweepstakes, polls, and other types of contests. It's important to note that Facebook has very strict guidelines around how contests can be conducted on the site, and they do require that you use a Facebook-approved app to manage the process. Since rules on Facebook tend to change often, be sure to check for the latest guidelines before you launch anything: https://www.facebook.com/page_guidelines.php.

Types of Prizes to Give Away

- Copies of your book or ebook

- Copies of books donated by fellow authors

- Prizes donated by partners and sponsors

- Downloadable information products (recordings, workbooks, etc.)

- Consulting time with you

- Access to an event you are hosting

- Gift cards or credit from a participating sponsor

- Big, enticing prizes like an iPad or laptop

- Trips and cruises, which can often be donated by a travel agency

It's always nice to generate contributions from sponsors, but you may also have to pony up some valuable prizes in order to make your contest exciting enough for people to not only enter, but to want to tell their friends about it.

Paid Advertising

Another option for getting your book in front of potential buyers is paid advertising. You can purchase ad space online and in print publications. The tricky part is finding the right opportunity that actually produces a decent return on investment (ROI). Because profit margins are low with books, it can be difficult to justify the cost of advertising. The goal with any marketing that you do should be to generate enough ROI to justify the cost. However, marketing involves a lot of testing to figure out what works best for the product you want to sell, so it can be worthwhile to dedicate a small budget to try out various advertising methods.

There are countless options for advertising in print publications. Major glossy magazine ads can cost tens of thousands of dollars. A more affordable option is to look for smaller niche publications like trade association newsletters, local weekly or monthly publications, and other small newspapers and industry journals. You will need to do some research to find publications that reach your target audience and decide whether it's worthwhile to test out an ad or two. With print advertising, repeat exposure is important. I wouldn't recommend running a single ad. You'll likely see better results if you run the same ad in the same publication several times in a row.

You can also look for advertising options on industry websites. If you come across a site that reaches your ideal audience, look for advertising guidelines or inquire with the site owner. You might be able to get some really affordable ad space as online ads often cost far less than print advertising.

Google Ads

Google's Adwords program (www.google.com/adwords) is an advertising network where you can bid on clicks for your ads. You do this by designating keywords that you want your ad associated with, and you can also target geographic locations and other demographics. For example, if your book is about caring for a puppy, your keywords might include "how to care for a new puppy" or "what to feed a puppy." Then, when a user searches Google for a similar phrase, your ad would appear at the top of the search results in the advertising section. If the user clicks on your ad, you will be charged for that click.

Bids for clicks can range from $.25 to several dollars PER click. Popular search phrases, like topics in the real estate or legal industries, can be quite expensive. However, less popular key phrases can cost far less.

When you set up an ad campaign, Google will show you suggested keyword phrases along with their popularity and estimate cost per click so it's easy to research your options. Google also maintains a content network, so your ads can appear on websites that display Google ads. That means that your puppy care book could potentially get featured on websites about dogs and puppies.

You can set virtually any budget you like with Google, so for as little as $50 you can test out an ad. I have yet to hear of any major author success stories with ads like these, but if you have a niche book topic and you're careful with your ad placement, these could produce some decent results for you. I would also recommend that you link your ad to a sales page on your own site so that you have control over the content that the user will see. Make sure you write a really compelling sales page to capture the interest of the buyers you have targeted.

It is also recommended that you try split testing, which means that you create multiple ads and multiple landing pages to test out which perform the best. This requires quite a bit of extra effort on your part, but if you think ads can work for you then it may be worthwhile.

Ads on the other search engines work in similar ways and can also cost less due to less competition so you may also want to test ads with the other search engines:

Bing: http://bingads.microsoft.com/
Yahoo: http://advertising.yahoo.com/
AOL: http://advertising.aol.com/

Facebook Ads

Similar to Google ads, Facebook ads (https://www.facebook.com/advertising) can be purchased on a pay-per-click basis, based on keywords and demographic information. Ads appear on Facebook users' pages, in the right sidebar, and include an image that you specify (such as your book cover).

Facebook ads can also be pricey. Depending on the size of the market you want to reach, suggested bid prices can range from $.75 up to $2 or more. The nice thing about Facebook ads is that you get a lot of impressions (views of your ad) before you have to pay for clicks. Your ad might get served up on 5,000 or 10,000 pages before someone actually clicks. That's a lot of visibility for your book cover and you only pay for the clicks.

Like all forms of advertising, you won't really know if it works until you test it out. If you can afford a budget of $50 or $100 for a month, this may be worth a try.

Promoted Posts

Because Facebook only displays your individual posts in the timelines of just 10% to 20% of your followers, each post you share misses out on a lot of visibility. In my opinion, Facebook did this on purpose to force small businesses to invest in promoting their posts, which ensures that more of your audience sees an individual post.

Under any given post on your Facebook business page, you will see a button for "Promote." You can choose to promote the post to people who like your page as well as to their friends. You can set a budget of as little as $5, which will ensure your post is seen by around 1,000 people in their timelines. The more you spend, the more visibility your post will receive.

Facebook has a lot of quirky rules around advertising with promoted posts. For example, the image that is included with your post cannot contain more than 20% text. If you post a logo that is text-based, your ad will likely get declined. So far it appears that books can still get approved under this system, however.

These ads can be effective in raising visibility for your book and other promotions that you feature on your page, and because the cost is low, it's worthwhile to take them for a test drive.

Advertising on Twitter and LinkedIn

Twitter now offers advertising: https://business.twitter.com/advertise/start/ or http://ads.twitter.com. With Twitter, you can currently participate in three different advertising options:

Promoted Tweets

The Promoted Tweets feature will increase visibility for a tweet that you designate, and can be amplified through Twitter search (your promoted tweet will appear in related search results), in the timelines for your followers (ensuring your followers see your tweet), in the timelines for people who are like your followers, but not actually following you. You can also promote tweets to mobile users.

For example, you could create a tweet about your book that looks like this:

New book for authors! The Nonfiction Book Marketing Plan by @bizauthor Bonus downloads when you buy: <link>

For promoted tweets, you will only pay when a user engages with the tweet by replying, clicking, or marking it as a favorite. Because there isn't yet a lot of competition for ads on Twitter, your bid rate will likely be lower than rates on Google and Facebook. If you want to get exposure for your book on Twitter, give promoted tweets a try. As with other advertising options, you can set a daily budget and cancel your ad at any time.

Promoted Accounts

Twitter's promoted accounts feature will raise visibility for your Twitter account, helping to attract more followers for your profile. This can be another way to gain followers on Twitter, though the cost can add up so only use this if you have a substantial budget. I prefer to be more proactive in building a Twitter following by going out and following other users on Twitter.

Promoted Trends

This advertising feature on Twitter will place your ad in the top ten trending topics on Twitter. Sounds great, right? Well, put your credit card away. This is an advertising level targeted toward large companies, and rumor has it that it costs upwards of $100k per DAY to participate.

LinkedIn Advertising

LinkedIn also offers advertising on the site (www.linkedin.com/advertising), though their ads are text based and clicks are pricey. From my own experience with LinkedIn ads, they don't perform nearly as well as other types of ads. I would only recommend testing this out if your book is business-oriented.

Author Interview

Name: William Teie

Website: http://DeerValleyPress.com

Books:

- *Leadership for the Wildland Fire Officer: Leading in a Dangerous Profession*

- *Firefighter's Handbook on Wildland Firefighting: Strategy, Tactics and Safety, 3rd Edition*

- *Study Guide for the Firefighter's Handbook on Wildland Firefighting, 3rd Edition*

- *Wildland Firefighting Fundamentals, 2nd edition*

- *4 Wheeler's Guide to the Rubicon Trail*
- *4 Wheeler's Guide: Trails of the Tahoe National Forest*
- *4 Wheeler's Guide: Trails of the San Bernardino Mountains*
- *History of a Place Called Rescue*

Are you traditionally published or self-published, and why did you make that choice?

After I retired as Fire Chief from the California Department of Forestry, I noticed that books dealing with wild land firefighting were outdated. I decided I would write a book and many people suggested I self-publish. Then I met Dan Poynter, author of *The Self-Publishing Manual*, and went to two seminars about self-publishing at his home in Santa Barbara. From that point on, I never looked back. I now have 12 titles, most of which are still in print, and have sold over 100,000 books.

My company, Deer Valley Press, was formed in 1994 and has been successful because I found an open niche and filled it. The lead title, *The Firefighter's Handbook*, is used worldwide as a college textbook and is in its 20th printing.

Tell us a bit about your most recent book:

I ventured out three years ago and wrote a history book about where I live: *A Place Called Rescue*. It is full color, 400+ pages, and costs $25,000 to print in China. (I don't really want to print in China, but you can't beat the price on color books.) But the project has paid for itself and I'm still selling quite a few. At Christmas time I advertised and sold about 200. The cover price is $75, but I usually sell it for less than $50. It was a fun project and won several prominent awards, including the Ben Franklin Award in 2012.

Who is your target audience of readers?

The target is firefighters that want to get a basic knowledge of wild land firefighting, plus fire departments and community colleges. At one point there were 60 community colleges nationwide that were buying it, though that has ebbed and flowed with the economy.

When the book hit the market in 1994 there was more acceptance of the fact that firefighters would purchase it on their own at full price. But when I started selling to colleges, and then Amazon came along, it was a rude awakening to take 55% off the cover price for retailers, so my margin dropped off steeply. But I fill orders to Amazon every week and consider it part of the cost of doing business.

What has been the single most effective marketing strategy you have used for promoting your book?

I had been in the fire service for a long time and had good name recognition in the U.S., so I called my friends and asked for mailing lists for all the firefighters they knew. I spent countless hours typing up those lists for direct mail campaigns. Eventually I had a website built, but started by mailing out postcards.

One of the other lessons I learned is that you always have to protect your wholesalers and never want to burn them. Early on I was selling books to the Firefighter Bookstore in Los Angeles County, which at the time was owned by Peggy Glen. One time she found out I was bidding a purchase that she was also bidding on and she called me up and said, "You really need to take care of your distributors." Later, I was going to sell about $3,000 worth of books to a county fire department, but they didn't want to purchase direct and so I gave them Peggy's name. She under-bid me, and then called and asked me to drop-ship the order. I did everything else and she made a lot of money. But that relationship I built with her was far more valuable over the long run.

What are some other marketing tactics that have or haven't worked for you?

One of the things that Dan Poynter said to me was pick a genre and stay there. This is very important. I ventured off years ago and wrote three trail guides for off-road enthusiasts. I love maps and though I'm not an off-roader, I love adventure. But writing those books forced me to focus on a whole other market. That more than doubled the work and the marketing. The other mistake I made was I didn't really research my market. I printed 10,000 copies of the first trail guide and had to dispose of about 3,000 copies.

One fun thing that happened along the way was an email I received from someone in South Africa. He operated a private firefighting agency, which was contracted by local land owners. They had a copy of my book and invited me to come for a visit and help them with their training efforts.

When I got there, I met with the president of the major technical university in South Africa and learned about what they needed. I came home and wrote a book for the southern hemisphere, which I accomplished by changing one of my books. It was an interesting project because I even had to change the English because they spell things differently. Basically I took the American out of English.

When it was done, I took the book back and spent a month in South Africa. I set it up with the Society of African Forests. They handled the printing and provided me royalties for five years. I requested that after five years they stop paying me royalties and put the money in a scholarship fund. The book is now in its second edition, fourth or fifth printing, and is sold all over southern Africa. It's a major handbook at over 500 pages, and in addition to English, it has been translated into African and Zulu languages.

What have been some of the biggest benefits of publishing a book?

My books have provided travel to South Africa twice, additional income, and various adventures. For the first ten or twelve years, the books also gave me access to the fire service. I'd go to fire shows and keep in touch with my friends, which was fun since I was retired.

At one point along the way, a major publisher asked to buy rights to my book. They said, "We'd like for you to sell us the rights for the book, and then have you rewrite it in our format," which was similar to their other textbooks. I remembered that Peggy Glen told me about a fire chief who had been working with the same company so I called him. He told me about his book and how he had self-published, but then accepted an agreement for the big publisher to buy it. After he went through the trouble of rewriting, they rejected it. When he said they couldn't do that, they told him to read his contract. He had no rights.

That's not something you forget. So I went out and hired a lawyer, and we started negotiating back and forth. Financially they couldn't compete with someone who didn't have overhead and also had a retirement income. We decided to go forward with it and I gave them a list of requests. They sent me a new agreement and I read it very carefully and if I'd have signed it, I wouldn't have any rights. So I called it off, yet they still call me about every six months asking if I'm ready to sell. Lesson learned: don't trust anyone; read the contracts.

What advice would you offer to new authors who are getting ready to promote their books?

Understand who you want to sell your books to. All of my books have been priced by Peggy Glen. I called her and described each book and she suggested the price. She'd look at her shelves to find what was comparable, and then would price it under by a couple bucks. You've got to price it to sell. Unless your last name is King or Clancy, publishing may or may not put you in a higher tax bracket, and you've got to sell your books. You might have a publisher, but you've still got to be the one to sell it.

The best thing to do is build a marketing package around your book. Create a PowerPoint presentation, give presentations and sell books. Unless you really know your market, your niche, and have access to the people who are going to buy it, then presentations are a great way you can get out in front of people.

If you were starting over today, is there anything you would do differently?

No, I don't think so. I'd want to make a couple of mistakes because it keeps you humble. I might not have done the trail guides. It took up capital and storage. That's the big difference between self-publishing and having a publisher. You have to be willing to spend some money. With ebooks today, it's not a big issue. You just need to invest your time and don't have to worry about printing and stocking.

I also sell study guides, which support the basic text from the main book, so they are companion guides. I have several add-on products, including a PowerPoint slide deck with over 2,000 slides that teaches the whole book and is delivered on DVD. Over the years I've also maintained a file called "other stuff." Whenever I saw a new report come out, I'd put it in my master file. That's another companion product that I sell, and it's always being updated. People love all that extra stuff. And if I can get an instructor to use it, then I've locked in their business. I sell it for $50 and often times I give it away because it leads to future sales.

Is there anything else you would like to add?

Publishing is fun and you can make some money at it if you're willing to take a risk. Be sure to always get an editor and a proofreader. I usually have my books proofed by two people. But even doing that, I have never printed a book that didn't have an error, which I usually discover within fifteen minutes of receiving them. That's just the way it is.

Chapter 9:
Professional Speaking

"There are always three speeches for every one you actually gave. The one you practiced, the one you gave, and the one you wish you gave."
– Dale Carnegie

AT SOME POINT IN YOUR author career, you will likely be invited to speak at an event. Though it may be among people's top fears—next to the fear of flying and ahead of the fear of death—public speaking has many advantages. As the featured speaker at an event, conference or meeting, you are perceived as the ultimate authority in the room. Speakers have a tremendous amount of influence with an audience, which removes a great barrier from purchasing your books, products, and services. The best news of all? As an author, it will be far easier for you to land speaking gigs because your book establishes your authority and opens those doors!

How to Break Into Professional Speaking

The easiest way to get started with speaking is to reach out to local trade associations, charitable and service groups like Kiwanis and Rotary, schools, chambers of commerce, retirement communities, and other organized groups. There are dozens, if not hundreds, of trade organizations in every major city that need speakers for their weekly or monthly meetings. That's right, they *need* speakers. As someone who has been in charge of running numerous groups in my community over the years, it is always difficult to find speakers because not enough people make an effort to reach out. That equals opportunity for you!

Another option is to teach classes at your local adult learning centers, parks and recreation departments, and community education programs. Even if only 10 students register for your class, you will still be promoted in their catalog, which is often sent to tens of thousands of people. The same is true for trade associations and organized groups. For example, a trade association with 800 members may only get 60 people to attend the monthly meeting, but as the speaker your information and bio is promoted to all 800 members.

Here are the steps to getting on the speaking circuit:

1. **Write a Great Description** – Be sure to write a brief and interesting description of your presentation, including three to five bullets explaining the benefits for the audience. The description of your presentation is often an important deciding factor in getting you booked for an engagement, and it's also commonly copied into event promotions and agendas.

2. **Develop a Speaker One-Sheet** – Most professional speakers have a one-page flyer that they can give to potential event hosts as a way to promote their speaking topics. Your sheet should include a brief overview of one or more speaking topics, testimonials from past presentations if you have them, a list of past audiences if available, your photo, book cover, and contact information.

3. **Add a Speaker Page to Your Website** – Take the information from your speaker sheet and add it to a page on your website. This effort alone can attract opportunities to speak! Also, if you want to graduate to paid speaking, it's essential that you include video clips of previous speaking engagements here.

4. **Start Reaching Out** – There are countless opportunities to speak in your own backyard. Spend some time on Google and look for trade associations, business groups, service groups, schools, chambers of commerce, and companies that reach your target audience. Start sending emails to contacts letting them know you're available to speak, and send along your speaker sheet. Remember that some organizations need speakers on a weekly basis for their meetings. Most will be quite glad to hear from you.

5. **Spread the Word** – Let your clients, peers, and friends know that you're available to speak. Ask if they know of any organizations that could benefit from your presentation.

6. **Build on Your Experience** – As you gain more experience, ask for testimonials from event coordinators and add them to your speaker sheet and website. Also, look for ways to have some of your

presentations recorded so that you have video clips to share on your website and offer to prospects. Sometimes events hosts already have plans to have a videographer in-house, and all you need to do is ask for a copy. Or, you can hire a local videographer or even a student from a local college to come film your event.

7. **Expand Your Offerings** – As you gain experience, add additional presentation topics to your menu of options. This will allow you to return to past clients and book another engagement, plus it can give you reasons to capture new opportunities.

Give Great Presentations

While you may think you have good public speaking skills, that doesn't always mean that you will dazzle an audience. Professional speakers spend years developing and refining their craft. At the very least, you should put some effort into cultivating your skills so that you leave your audience with a great impression. Here's how:

1. **Develop a Powerful Speech** – Captivating an audience involves giving a great presentation. It should never be directly about your book or your business, but instead about *a topic of interest to your audience.* Teach them something, entertain them, and tell plenty of stories. Great speaking is all about telling interesting stories and giving examples the audience can relate to.

2. **Practice Your Presentation** – Years ago I worked as a trainer for a software company and we were taught to practice our presentations in an empty room, over and over again. This is how you refine your skills, learn your material, and show up polished and prepared. If you're really brave, video tape yourself and watch it back. You'll discover that you sway side to side, talk too fast, jingle change in your pocket, and have other habits that distract from your message.

3. **Use Props Carefully** – Sometimes props can add visual interest, but avoid anything too gimmicky. I once watched a business speaker juggle scarves. It didn't fit the theme of the presentation, was distracting, and left the entire room looking a little uncomfortable. On the other hand, visual props that illustrate a point can enhance your presentation. If the audience is small enough, when I speak about

information products I sometimes bring along examples and pass them around the room. When in doubt, leave props out.

4. **Create Compelling Slides** – Your PowerPoint slides are meant to enhance your presentation, not *be* your presentation. Avoid the urge to load your slides with text. Generally speaking, you should keep text to a minimum and no more than five bullet items per slide. When possible, use an image to illustrate a point instead of text. For timing purposes, a good rule to follow is to estimate two to three minutes per slide. So if you have a 60 minute presentation, you should only need 20 to 30 slides.

5. **Give Attendees Something to Keep** – I always bring along a handout with tips for the audience. My goal is to give them something they will want to keep long after the event is over, so that they can remember me later. At the bottom of the page, you can include a brief bio and contact information.

6. **Respect the Time Allotted** – It's better to finish early than late. When you run over your time, you risk losing the audience's attention, especially if they are anticipating a break or if they are ready to move along to the next session. If you finish early, you can open the floor for questions. It's also a good idea to bring along some bonus material or discussion points in case you're unsure of timing and need some filler at the end.

7. **Consider a Giveaway** – One easy way to collect contact information from attendees is to raffle off a copy of your book at the end of your presentation. I like to bring along a small gift bag with handles and pass it around the room about halfway through my presentation so that attendees have learned a bit about me and my style. At the end, I will make a big deal of drawing a winner for the book. Then, I'll remind attendees that I'll be available to sign books at my table after the event.

8. **Give Thanks** – Remember to send the event coordinator a thank you note! Hopefully you will be invited back again at a later date and also referred to speak at other events.

You might be surprised by how quickly you can sell more books and grow your business as a result of your speaking engagements. Soon you may find that you don't have to go looking for speaking opportunities. As you build a reputation, the invitations to speak will come to you. And after you do enough free speaking, you will inevitably find opportunities for paid speaking engagements. These can range from a stipend of $50 up to thousands of dollars once you establish your authority in your field!

AUTHOR TIP: For more dynamic presentations, check out Prezi (http://prezi.com), which is a cloud-based solution for creating presentation slides that also function like a whiteboard.

Transition to Paid Speaking

If you want speaking to become a revenue stream for you, start by getting as many free engagements under your belt as possible. Then begin reaching out to companies and conferences that need speakers. Professional speakers typically earn $2,500 to $10,000 and up for a keynote presentation, plus travel expenses. It can be a lucrative career, though one that takes time and effort to build. Here are some additional tips for paid speaking:

1. **Ask for Payment** – Once you have some experience, simply decide to start asking for payment. Small associations and many conference break-out sessions won't pay, but larger events and companies will *expect* to pay you. Most importantly, it never hurts to ask. You will still end up speaking for free at some events—most speakers do— but when you start to request fees, you might be surprised to actually earn them! A good starting rate is between $2,500 to $5,000. It may sound high, but it's the going rate for speakers. You can also negotiate fees and travel expenses. If a company has a tight budget, you can reduce your fee. You might also try bartering for something in return. One speaker I know once got a brand new car to drive around for a full year in exchange for a one-hour keynote.

2. **Bundle in Books** – Some companies will gladly buy a copy of your book for all attendees. This usually comes out of a different budget than the speaker fee, and once again, it never hurts to ask.

3. **Update Your Speaker Page** – Add a note on the speaker page of

your website that sets the expectation that you charge a fee. Mine says: *"Please call or e-mail for speaker rates. A 50% deposit is required to reserve the date with the balance due on the day of the event. Special considerations may be made for non-profit organizations."*

4. **Network With Other Speakers** – The National Speakers Association (NSA) is the leading organization for speakers: http://nsaspeaker.org. Locally, I run the Sacramento Speaker's Network and we welcome new members: http://sacramentospeakersnetwork.com. There is also Toastmasters, where members practice their skills: http://toastmasters.org.

5. **Have Fun** – When you enjoy what you do, it comes across. It will take some practice, but when you find your passion for speaking it can have a powerful impact on building your personal brand and your bottom line.

Resources for Speakers

- www.Toastmasters.org – Find a chapter near you to learn the craft of speaking professionally
- http://www.nsaspeaker.org/ – National Speakers Association
- http://www.astd.org/ – American Society for Training and Development
- http://www.asla.com/ – American Seminar Leaders Association
- http://SpeakerNetNews.com – Free newsletter with subscriber tips for speakers

Books

- *Speak and Grow Rich* by Dottie Walters and Lilly Walters
- *The Wealthy Speaker* by Jane Atkinson
- *Money Talks: How to Make a Million as a Speaker* by Alan Weiss

AUTHOR TIP: If you have a PowerPoint presentation prepared, you can load your slides to SlideShare (http://www.slideshare.net/), a presentation sharing service that will give you some HTML code to add a side viewer widget to your speaker page. Note that you can also share your SlideShare presentations via Facebook and on your LinkedIn page. Why not give potential clients a preview?

Speaker Intake Form

When I receive an inquiry from someone who wants to hire me as a speaker for their event, I go through a series of questions to make sure I understand the scope of the opportunity. This Speaker Intake Form helps me collect all of the data I need to move forward and meet expectations for an event. Feel free to copy the details below, modify them to fit your needs, and create your own form!

Speaker Intake Form:

- Contact Name
- Name of Company or Event
- Phone
- Email
- Fax
- Mailing Address
- Speaking Topic
- Date and Time of Event
- Event Location (city, state, and hotel/venue)
- Length of Presentation Time
- Multiple Presentations Needed?

Audience Size

- Describe the audience. What do they do? What are their challenges? What do they want to learn/take away from this session?

- A/V equipment available?

- Will you film the event? (If so, request a copy)

- Internet access available?

- Vendor table available for book/product sales?

- Interested in purchasing books for audience?

- What is your budget for this presentation?

- What are the guidelines for travel budget and arrangements? Should I book the travel or will your company handle that?

- Onsite event contact name and cell phone number?

- Other Notes

Some Additional Considerations

If you're getting paid, you should ask if you can speak with several audience members prior to the event so that you can better understand their interests and needs. Also, speakers should collect a 50% deposit along with a signed contract in order to finalize arrangements for a speaking engagement. The balance due of 50% should be payable on or before the day of the event.

Download a copy of this intake form, plus a sample speaker contract here: http://nonfictionauthorsassociation.com/book-downloads/.

What You Can Learn from TED Speakers

One of my favorite things to do when I have some free time is to watch videos on TED.com. If you've somehow missed the TED phenomenon, you should know that the site features 20 minute presentations from some of the world's top thought leaders. Speakers for TED events are selected on an invite-only basis. You can learn a lot about being an effective professional speaker by watching these powerful videos.

Here are some of the lessons from the TED speakers:

Practice is Essential

Speakers for TED must keep their content to a maximum of 20 minutes, which is incredibly hard for most of us to do. Because of this, most speakers *practice* their presentations over and over again before stepping on stage, which ensures their content fits in the time allotted. Preparation also comes in handy if nerves kick in. When you are well-prepared and have most of your material memorized (or at least the opening and closing, which is what I personally try to do), your knees may shake a bit, but your brain will go on auto-pilot and you won't miss a beat.

Content Must Be Captivating

Storytelling is the most important element of an interesting presentation. All of the TED speakers tell interesting stories to engage the audience. Also, note that some use PowerPoint slides and when they do, only a few slides are used and they aren't overloaded with text. Simple is the name of the game here.

Must Have a Clear Purpose and Flow

Most of us are used to speaking for an hour, so when it comes to shrinking a presentation into one-third of its original size, it can be quite challenging. TED speakers know to first define a purpose for their content and then develop a logical flow of information, meaning the presentation has a beginning, middle, and an end. Like a good novel that reaches a climax, speakers should aim to do the same.

No Theatrics Needed

For years I struggled with the idea that I needed to be more theatrical on stage. There are many speakers, especially in the motivational speaker category, who really know how to put on a show. That might mean dancing around the stage, juggling, or dramatic gestures and physical movement. But I'm not a motivational speaker and these antics never felt authentic for me.

Watching the TED videos was a great reminder that speakers don't have to get on stage and put on a show. In fact, an authentic audience connection is *far more important*, and you can see this as a common thread throughout the TED site.

I recently put this theory to the test when I gave a presentation at the annual National Speakers Association conference. Talk about pressure—I was scheduled to speak to a room full of professional speakers! After my session, which had about 100 attendees, the feedback was overwhelming. They loved the content, but more importantly, I received many compliments about my authentic and engaging style. I have settled into a comfortable place where

I deliver content with passion and without fanfare. It seems to be working. Most TED speakers follow the same recipe.

By the way, rumor has it that the TED organizers will open up the opportunity for speakers to apply to speak on the influential TED stage soon. Watch for more details as they are announced!

Author Interview

Name: Heidi BK Sloss

Website: www.heidisloss.com

Books:

- *Fortune is in the Follow-Up®: 5 Power Strategies to Reinvent Your Marketing*
- *10 Powerful Women®: 10 Strategic Insights into Successful Business* (co-author)

Are you traditionally published or self-published, and why did you make that choice?

I chose to be traditionally published because it helps builds my credibility. The reason I wrote my book was to build my credibility as a business strategist and follow-up expert. When people hear me talk about my publisher, they have an immediate and positive reaction. There is a real perception that a book must be better or at least have some qualitative substance if a publisher was involved.

Tell us a bit about your most recent book:

I just reissued Fortune is in the Follow-Up®'s second edition. It is a back-to-basics business how-to book, teaching business owners and independent sales agents my five power strategies to help them reinvent their marketing. The premise of the book is that marketing is all about building strong relationships with prospects until they want to do business. Each strategy teaches readers how to leverage their time, energy and resources to make the most of their relationship building.

Who is your target audience of readers?

Business owners and independent sale agents.

What has been the single most effective marketing strategy you have used for promoting your book?

At first it was having a book launch strategy that helped make *Fortune is in the Follow-Up®* a best-seller: being able to claim my book as a best-seller is a great cache. Secondary is that I interviewed industry experts for stories and case studies. People are interested in reading what those experts had to say. Additionally people buy copies of books in which they appear.

What are some other marketing tactics that have or haven't worked for you?

Some other tactics that have worked well for me:

- Landing a great radio interview with a well-known radio show on the eve of my book launch.

- Putting out the 2nd edition with a better cover--it has since been picked up in the latest Bakers and Taylor Catalogue.

- At the moment I am using a book marketing service that has put the book out to reviewers to be placed on a variety of blogs. Am hopeful about this one.

- Using video to create book trailers for both editions that have been easily shared on a variety of social media forums.

Some tactics that have not worked well for me:

- I hired a public relations expert and while I learned some useful information, it was not worth the expense.

- I attended the BEA in New York City and it was not worth the expense for the little good it did me.

How has social media impacted your success? Which social media networks do you feel generate the best results for you?

I have been using Facebook, Linked-In, YouTube and Twitter to create buzz and raise my profile. Can't say that I can point to one in particular that has sold more books than the others. But I did make a contact, on Facebook, because of my book, that has been worth about $8000 to me so far. I look at social media marketing, like other strategies as long-term relationship building ones.

What have been some of the biggest benefits of publishing a book?

Biggest benefits: built-in credibility, brand awareness, higher profile, better self-confidence, many more paid speaking engagements.

What advice would you offer to new authors who are getting ready to promote their books?

Start marketing your book right away. Don't wait for it to be done before you start promoting it and you. I had a hard time with this, but I can see that the relationships I built, trying to promote my book before it was done, have paid off. Start promoting and talking about your book right away. Have a title and then use the title to build buzz and excitement. Have a great cover created as soon as possible. And don't skimp on the cover. Having had two different covers for what is essentially the same book, people have a much better and strong reaction to a better cover. Also, I used my cover to promote the book, generate interest and attract industry experts to participate in my interviews. Without the cover it would not have been as successful.

If you were starting over today, is there anything you would do differently?

I am very happy with the way things have turned out for me since conceiving and writing my book. I wouldn't want to change any of the things that I have learned from the process.

Is there anything else you would like to add?

Writing a book has been the single most effective way for me to grow my business. I recommend it to anyone who is running a business these days. Business cards and website are good to have, but without a book, it is very hard to get noticed.

Chapter 10:
Revenue Generation

"The more that you read, the more things you will know. The more that you learn, the more places you'll go."
– Dr. Seuss

A BOOK IS A FANTASTIC credibility-builder and can create a wide variety of opportunities for authors. While the book itself can generate some revenues, the real profits often come from the other revenue-generating activities that you create around the book.

Consulting and Coaching

Writing a nonfiction book based on your area of expertise is an easy lead-in for consulting and coaching opportunities. In fact, these opportunities will probably come looking for you whether you want them or not!

After I wrote my first book, *The Business Startup Checklist and Planning Guide*, I began receiving requests for consulting services. This wasn't something I had planned on since at the time I was running my bookstore and building my business website and it never really occurred to me. But readers were looking for additional assistance and it made perfect sense to begin offering consulting services.

Over the years I've discussed this option with many authors and have been surprised by some of the resistance. It seems that some authors feel they aren't qualified to call themselves consultants or coaches. But here's the thing: You wrote an entire book about your topic of interest. In the eyes of readers, that makes you an expert. And experts typically offer some form of consulting service! Also, avoid comparing yourself with others. That will get you nowhere fast. Clearly you have a lot to say about your topic and you have every right to own that. You may not have ALL of the answers, but you know more than most people.

The other important lesson I've learned over the years that even though your book might provide all the steps needed for your readers to accomplish something, many will still want accountability and personal support. We retain a very small percentage of the information we learn every day so many of your readers will want reinforcement. They will want you to help them along the path you've laid out before them.

Start by considering what kinds of programs you want to offer to your clients. There are two primary ways to offer your services:

Consulting by the hour – This is pretty standard in the consulting and coaching industry, though it lacks flair and I personally prefer to offer consulting packages. In this case you simply bill clients on an hourly basis, similar to how an attorney charges for his time. If you go this route, be sure to charge a competitive rate for your services. Just because you're new to consulting, that doesn't mean you should charge less than your competitors. You are an authority after all. I also suggest setting a minimum commitment level for clients, such as two or five hours. Filling your schedule with random one-hour client sessions can quickly feel like drudgery, especially if those clients aren't encouraged to return anytime soon.

Consulting packages – This is my favorite option, both as a consumer and a consultant. You can design packages in any number of ways, specifically to meet the needs of your audience.

Your packages might simply be based on the time you commit to spending with the client. Many life coaches sell their services based on 90-day, 6-month, or even 12-month packages, which include weekly or bi-monthly coaching calls.

Your packages might also be created for some specific purpose. For years one of my bestselling packages was a Marketing Action Plan, which included a two-hour consultation with the client, a written action plan sent to the client after the session, and a follow-up call a month later to check on the client's progress. Over the years I charged between $1,000 and $3,000 for these plans.

Another option is to offer your clients full-day visits with you, which would be considered a premium package and should be billed accordingly. When I owned my bookstore, I received many inquiries from people who were interested in opening stores in their own towns across the country. At that time I charged $5,000 for a full-day consultation, allowing clients to follow along to learn all about the store operations.

Jason Davis, who is known as "The Dog Guy" and co-owner of the Folsom Dog Resort, offers a similar program to other dog training facilities. Companies pay substantial fees to send their staff to Jason for training programs that last one to three weeks, where Jason teaches them his dog training techniques and participants also learn about the business operations.

Your consulting packages can be presented in any way that you like. You might bundle up some books and workbooks for your clients as part of a package, or create a formal program that walks clients through a process week-by-week until they reach the end of the program. Get creative and figure out what your clients want.

Live Workshops and Training Classes

If you enjoy teaching, then workshops and training classes may be a great option for you. Similar to consulting packages, you can develop your programs in just about any way that you choose. The simplest option, and a good place to start, is to create a half-day event, which would be a three- or four-hour workshop. Workshops should be interactive and engage participants, since most people don't want to sit through three hours of lecture. Include questions and answers with the audience, group sharing of their experiences, and exercises that participants can do either individually or in small groups.

A full-day workshop is a bigger commitment and you'll need to include plans for handling meals. You can bring food in for your students, or give them enough time for an extended lunch break on their own.

Multi-day workshops can be quite lucrative. Alicia Dunams is a book coach who runs a workshop called "Bestseller in a Weekend," where participants spend a full weekend writing a first draft of a book. Some additional services are bundled in with the registration fee, including editing, book cover design, and interior layout for the book.

You can also take the workshop concept a step further and host a conference, which usually consists of a multi-day event with several speakers. Conferences can have additional revenue streams when you sell vendor tables and related advertising, plus on-site bookstore sales, and additional offers. I recently attended a Tony Robbins event, which featured several of Tony's own business entities in the vendor area offering all kinds of additional items for attendees to purchase, ranging from books and T-shirts to five-figure coaching programs. There is a lot of money to be made from events.

Webinars, Teleseminars, and Online Events

You can take advantage of technology to deliver educational programs around the globe. Webinars and teleseminars are events conducted online or by phone. With a teleseminar, participants dial in to a conference line to listen in on an instructional program or interview, and often participate in Q&As. With webinars, participants can view an online presentation, which can include a PowerPoint slide deck or a demonstration of some sort. With both types of events, you can extract recordings in MP3 format and sell them as digital downloads for years to come (or as long as the information is still relevant).

There are a lot of free teleseminars and webinars available online so if you want to charge for yours, make sure it is unique and has a higher perceived value than the free ones. One way to earn income from these events is to offer some kind of series, such as a four- or six-week course delivered via teleseminar or webinar.

Hay House publishing also hosts many online classes throughout the year, conducted by its expert authors. Participants typically pay from $49 to $149 for a series of teleclasses, and an exclusive forum is set up so that participants can ask questions and engage with each other. Note that forums typically work best when you have a lot of participants and can't accommodate many live audience questions. Hay House has been around for a long time and has a large following, so often times these classes have hundreds of participants. And if you do the math, these are quite lucrative. I once paid $99 for one of their courses, which had over 300 participants—that adds up to around $30,000 in revenue generated for one four-week class. Not too shabby, eh?

Another model you can develop is a self-study course, where you provide access to training lectures via MP3 recordings, webinar playback, or video modules. In a course like this, students should also receive some specific exercises and steps to follow as they work through the course.

The big kahuna of online events is online conferences, which like training classes, can be conducted via teleseminar, webinar, or video streaming.

Online conferences function much like an in-person conference, without the headaches of travel and food and venue expenses.

I host an annual online conference for nonfiction authors: http:// NonfictionWritersConference.com. This event is held over three days in May each year, with 15 expert speakers presenting lectures from around the globe. We conduct five sessions per day via teleseminar and attendees have the option to participate live or download recordings and transcripts. We also make handouts available via download, and offer bonuses just for signing up. This is a fun and lucrative event each year. I also enjoy the added benefit of reaching out to invite speakers. I've made many industry friends as a result of hosting this conference, and many also help to promote the event to their networks each year.

Whatever format you choose, online events can be effective, fun, and profitable. They are also quite cost-effective and can be turned into information products that you can continue selling long after the event is over.

Certification Programs

Another exciting revenue-generating strategy is to create a certification program. In this case, you would develop a training program and participants would complete some sort of test at the end in order to be considered certified in your program.

Jim Horan, author of *The One Page Business Plan*, has built a brilliant business around his book. He offers certification programs to consultants who want to teach his methods, transforming them into agents who promote his brand and his books as certified One Page Business Plan consultants. Participants invest several thousand dollars to go through the online course and complete the certification program, and then are sent out to teach Horan's methods all over the world. He's not the only author to do this. Michael Gerber, Michael Port, and John Jantsch all offer similar programs.

Jan B. King is a publishing consultant who developed a certification program for virtual assistants to become certified authors' assistants (http:// www.authorsassistanttraining.com/). Participants learn strategies for helping authors promote their books, and in return they receive a certification to put on their career *résumés* and get listed in an online directory: http://authorsassistants.com/ (by the way, this is a great place to find an assistant).

You will find all kinds of certification programs out there, and if you can find a need within your target audience, you can certainly create a program of your own.

Information Products

As an author, you can produce information products that complement the subject matter of your books, and then sell those products to readers for passive income. You can also use them for marketing purposes to attract new readers for your books or distribute as bonus items for new newsletter subscribers, event attendees, or in conjunction with a new book launch.

Information products can be offered in a variety of formats:

Ebooks – Thanks to the influx of digital readers, ebooks are hotter than ever. You can make an ebook available through your website as a PDF document (which I highly recommend as people will still purchase PDFs), plus have it formatted for Kindle, Nook, iPad, etc. One distribution option is http://Smashwords.com, which is a cost-effective way to convert and distribute ebooks to all the major retailers except Amazon. For our clients at Authority Publishing, we recommend a combination of formatting for Amazon (http://kdp.amazon.com) and Smashwords to cover all bases.

Many writers are also earning funds by distributing niche ebooks, which are oftentimes shorter than a standard ebook. For example, if you're a divorce attorney in Texas, you could produce an ebook called "How to Get a Divorce in Texas: A Woman's Guide to Getting What You Deserve." If this topic isn't already covered, you could easily find an audience for this niche topic.

Workbooks – I often wonder why more authors don't create workbooks as companion products for their books. If your book teaches how to do something, why not create a workbook to help readers put the lessons into action? Workbooks give the reader something more to do and can add value to a reader's experience. They are relatively easy to create and can give a nice boost to your revenues. Here are some more reasons to consider adding a workbook to your product list:

- Workbooks are a natural up-sell to a nonfiction book.
- Readers will appreciate having an interactive experience with your content.

- Workbooks have a higher perceived value. Typical prices range from $20 to $35.

- You can bundle a workbook with your book to increase back-of-the-room sales.

- Workbooks are easier to write than books because there is less content and more white space.

- In addition to a printed version, you can sell your workbook as a PDF download, cutting costs and increasing profits.

- The PDF version of your workbook can be given away as a bonus with other purchases.

- Workbooks can be great tools for working with consulting clients.

- For workshops, workbooks add tremendous value for participants while also making your job as workshop leader easier.

- A workbook doesn't have to be spiral bound; it can be perfect bound and put into distribution like any other book on Amazon and other retail outlets.

What to include in your workbook:

- Simple, supporting text to explain exercises
- Fill in the blanks
- Essay questions
- Worksheets
- Spreadsheets
- Thoughtful questions that the reader can answer
- Plenty of white space for writing

Special Reports – Shorter than an ebook, a special report can be two to fifty pages on a specific topic that would be hard to find elsewhere, delivered in PDF format. (Note that if you create a report that is greater than 50 pages, you can probably just call it an ebook and then format and sell it accordingly.)

Your reports can cover all kinds of topics. Years ago when my son was diagnosed with food allergies, I was up late one night searching for a list of dairy-free foods. I stumbled across a list that was sold by a nutritionist and I paid around $20 to download it in an Excel spreadsheet format. It was a quick and easy decision to make that purchase.

Reports can also teach specific industry-related strategies. Joan Stewart, known as the Publicity Hound (http://PublicityHound.com), has been selling short reports from her website for many years. Stewart's reports currently cost $15 each and cover PR-related topics, like how to pitch yourself to the media and how to create a media kit on a budget. While much of this information can be found online or in books, Stewart has built a strong and loyal following of people who are willing to spend a small amount for her advice. She also masterfully pitches her reports in her weekly newsletter by writing brief articles and then ending with, "If you liked this article, you'll love XYZ report where I share how to…"

Audio Recordings – As discussed earlier in this chapter, audio recordings should be delivered in MP3 format. These can be generated by hosting online classes, conferences, or even just with you sitting down at your desk and creating instructional materials.

Everything Else – An information product is basically any kind of information that you can package and deliver to buyers. You could develop white papers (which are like technical reports), transcripts of recordings, booklets, databases, formatted spreadsheets, worksheets, templates, audio or video recordings on a disk, or card decks.

Product Bundles – Keep the content train rolling by bundling together many of the items listed here. You could create packages that include your book, workbook, a ticket to your workshop, and an hour of consulting time. Get creative! Product bundles can be quite attractive, either as a one-time promotion or something that you also make available on an ongoing basis in your online store.

When it comes to information products, it's important the content meets a need for your audience. To increase your chances of success, start by doing a bit of research and planning prior to product development. Following are the steps you can take:

1. **Generate Product Ideas** - Start by listing the questions you are asked most often by your readers. If you find yourself answering the same questions repeatedly, consider that insight into potential product development opportunities. Also make a list of any topics that

you didn't cover in your books that you think readers would enjoy.

2. **Get Input from Your Target Audience** - Survey your *target* audience, not your friends or your family, but the people you most want to reach. Find out what needs they have that you can fill with the right product. You can use a tool such as http://SurveyMonkey.com to gather data.

3. **Evaluate Internet Search Demand** - Google's free keyword tool (https://adwords.google.com/o/KeywordTool) allows you to type in a key phrase and see the number of monthly searches conducted locally and globally. This tool also generates a list of related keywords, which can be a great way to inspire product ideas while determining demand for the products you create.

4. **Find a Market Need** - The best information products fill a need for the buyer, which means your product should solve a problem, provide how-to advice or reveal hard-to-find industry information. Also, a product that is too broad may have a harder time finding an audience versus one that is designed for a niche market. For example, if you're an author of a travel guide, instead of creating a report with general travel packing tips, you might create a series of reports with packing tips for specific destinations. For example, "Packing for Your Australian Vacation" or "Packing for Your Caribbean Cruise." Including a niche focus will help your audience connect with the product and will increase appeal for those who fit that need.

5. **Choose Your Format** - Decide if you are creating an ebook, special report, audio series, video series, workbook, or other type of information product.

6. **Establish the Right Price** - Every market is different and your price will depend on many factors: how much your audience can afford to pay, how much they want or need your information, scarcity of competition, your authority and reputation in your field, and perceived benefits of your offer. Also consider the perceived value of your product. A price that is too low may send the message that it won't be worthwhile, while a price that is too high may limit the number of purchases and raise expectations with those who do buy. For best results, test different pricing options to determine which will work best.

7. **Create a Great Sales Page** - I'm going to take a stand here and tell you that I despise long-form sales pages. I can also tell you that you can absolutely sell products without them. Instead, create a great, content-rich sales page that describes the benefits of your product, includes compelling testimonials (from real users who received an early sample copy, not friends or family!), establishes your authority as the product creator, and makes it easy to purchase.

8. **Automate Delivery** - Consumers buying online want instant gratification. Make sure you automate the purchase and delivery of your products using a shopping cart system such as http://ejunkie.com, http://oneshoppingcart.com, or http://payloadz.com.

9. **Promote, Promote, Promote** - You can have the best product on the planet, but if nobody knows about it, it won't matter. Make sure your product page is optimized for the search engines. Consider purchasing Google pay-per-click ads to test sales conversion. Cross-promote your product on your blog, social media sites, newsletter, speaking engagements, and everywhere else where you have the opportunity to reach your target audience. The more effort you put into it, the more rewards you will receive.

50 Ways to Transform Content into Information Products

1. Books

2. Mini-books (they don't all have to read like novels!)

3. Booklets

4. Ebooks

5. Special reports

6. White papers

7. Workbooks

8. Worksheets

9. Templates

10. Resource lists

11. Database of resources

12. Spreadsheets

13. Pre-formatted spreadsheet templates

14. Charts/graphs

15. Checklists

16. Statistics

17. Survey results

18. Blog posts

19. Articles

20. Case studies

21. Interviews

22. Compilations (stories, articles, interviews, case studies, etc.)

23. Videos (full-length)

24. Video clips

25. Video trailers

26. Audio recordings

27. Audio recording series

28. Podcasts

29. Teleseminars

30. Teleseminar series

31. Webinars

32. Webinar series

33. Transcripts

34. Electronic newsletters

35. Print newsletters

36. Print magazines

37. Web-based magazines

38. Comic strips

39. Games

40. Card decks

41. Short stories

42. Computer-based training

43. E-mail auto-responder series

44. iPhone apps

45. iPad apps

46. Sample chapters

47. Audio books

48. Licensed content (articles, graphics, etc. that others can repurpose)

49. Ring tones

50. Bundles (collection of several items as listed above)

AUTHOR TIP: You can allow others to sell your products as affiliates, which can often be accomplished with your shopping cart software (1shoppingcart.com or ejunkie.com). Another great option is ClickBank (http://clickbank.com), which is a marketplace for affiliates to find products to sell. List your products here and also consider selling other products as an affiliate.

Paid Freelance Writing

Many authors earn additional income from paid freelance writing, which has the added benefit of getting additional exposure for the author with the publication's readers. Getting paid to write for publications is a whole different ball game from writing free articles and distributing them to print and online publications purely for exposure. In order to get paid for your articles, you have to build on your experience and get the attention of editors. Print publications have pay ranges from $.25 per word up to $2 or more per word, depending on the distribution size of the publication. The top glossy magazines pay much higher rates than local newspapers and hometown magazines.

Start Small

It's not easy to break in to the large magazines that you see at the checkout stands in your grocery store. Most contributors for premium publications have many years of professional freelancing experience. However, you can work your way up to major publications if that is your goal, or you can choose to stick with writing for small and mid-size publications.

In chapter 7 I covered how to write for smaller publications by contributing article reprints or providing first rights. Once you have a few of those under your belt, you will officially have "clips," which is an industry term for samples of your work. Bigger publications will want to see these.

Write a Query

When it comes to writing for larger publications, the standard cost of admission is a query letter to the editor. A good query opens with a proposed story idea. That means you need to pitch something relevant for the publication's audience. It should briefly explain the angle you will take with the story, followed by why you are the best person to write the story. Here's a brief example of a pitch to a wedding industry business magazine:

> Dear <editor name>,
>
> Pinterest has quickly become the third largest social media site and I would like to write an article for <publication name> called "Pinterest Profits! How Wedding Professionals Can Turn Pins into Dollars." This article will explore how wedding professionals are leveraging Pinterest to increase website traffic and gain more customers. I will interview three sources who I have already identified and write a 1200-word article with concrete tips and solutions for your readers.
>
> I am an author of <book title> and I have written articles for <list publications here or leave this line out if no experience just yet>. You

can view some of my previous work here: <links to your articles from smaller industry publications>. I appreciate your consideration and would welcome the opportunity to work with you.

Sincerely,

Annie Author

A query should be brief, compelling (great title), timely (related to a hot trend or tied-in with an upcoming event or holiday), and should clearly appeal to the publication's target audience. To locate editors, look for an email address in the masthead or via the publication's website. Another great source for locating editorial contacts is Writer's Market, a paid directory: http:// writersmarket.com.

Bulk Sales

Selling books one at a time is a sure-fire way to generate enough money to fund your coffee habit, but selling them in large quantities can earn enough to actually pay some bills! Selling in bulk to non-bookstore markets can not only be lucrative, it can also minimize the headaches that come from distributing books via the typical bookstore model. In fact, selling books to bookstores is loaded with challenges.

To get a self-published book into bookstores, you will need to locate a book distributor. These are the folks that actually get books placed on bookstore shelves. Distributors will expect to purchase your books at 50% to 65% off of the retail price, leaving you with a very slim profit. And the worst thing about the bookstore industry is that books must be returnable. That way if the store fails to sell your books, they can return them at any time, in any condition, for a full refund. Selling to bookstores is one of the hardest ways authors can earn money.

The good news is that there are plenty of other places to sell your books in bulk, and you can do so without having to accept returns. Here are some options for bulk book sales:

- Large corporations can distribute your books at their events or tradeshows. Instead of a coffee mug, pen or other boring promotional item, they can give away your books!
- Companies can distribute books to their customers or employees.

When the book *Who Moved My Cheese* gained popularity, companies all over the U.S. bought thousands of copies to distribute to employees in an effort to help them embrace change.

- Co-brand your book with a non-profit by adding their logo to your cover, and have their corporate sponsor purchase copies to distribute to members.

- Retailers could give away your books as a bonus with purchase. For example, if you wrote a book on wellness with vitamins, convince your local drugstore to feature your book in the pharmacy department.

- Specialty retailers like gift shops, car washes, gas stations, etc. can stock your books for sale or give it away as a bonus with purchase.

- A local business might be thrilled to set up a large display of your books as a way to entice new customers. For example, a bank could give your business book away to new banking customers. After the promotion is successful in a local branch, ask to speak to someone at corporate headquarters who could approve the promotion across all branches.

- College professors often choose the books their students use for curriculum. Convince them to use yours and soon your books could be featured across dozens or even hundreds of college campuses.

Think big and you could ultimately generate some tremendous bulk sales as a result. For more information, pick up a copy of Brian Jud's book: *How to Make Real Money Selling Books (Without Worrying About Returns): A Complete Guide to the Book Publishers' World of Special Sales.*

AUTHOR TIP: If you've built a significant following on Twitter (10,000+ followers), you may actually be eligible to get paid for tweets by sponsors who want to reach your target audience. Celebrities earn tens of thousands of dollars for mentioning products in their tweets, and authors can earn a bit of cash, too (though probably not as much as Kim Kardashian). Check out http://SponsoredTweets.com to enroll as a paid tweeter. And don't worry, you will have the ability to screen and approve offers from sponsors. You may not get rich from sponsored tweets, but it can be a fun sideline income.

Smart Phone Apps

Thanks to ever-increasing market of smart phone users, apps (short for applications) have become incredibly popular, and for some, quite lucrative too. If you can create a niche app that hasn't already been done well by someone else, you can generate profits a few dollars at a time.

For example, if you wrote a book on how to live gluten-free, you could develop an app that works like a gluten dictionary, allowing users to look up foods and find out if they contain gluten. A life coach might create an app that delivers a daily meditation or journaling exercise. An author of a financial guide might create a money tracker app.

Whatever you choose, having an app developed might not be as complicated or as expensive as it sounds. A good source for finding developers is http://odesk.com. You can put out a request for bids and find a software developer with a high score from previous users. A friend of mine recently had a fairly complex app developed for under $1,000. It can be done if this is something you'd like to do.

Corporate Sponsors

One big benefit of being an author and cultivating an audience is that you can attract corporate sponsors. This essentially means that corporations will give you money to help them reach your audience.

I have personally worked with over a dozen corporate sponsors in recent years and have earned well into the six figures from those relationships. For me it all began with my website: BusinessInfoGuide.com, which provides resources for entrepreneurs. I launched the site back in 2004 with the goal of attracting my target audience of readers by sharing useful information. As the site grew over time, and I positioned myself as an authority, offers for corporate sponsorships began showing up. It felt a bit like finding a pot of gold at the end of the rainbow.

The harsh reality is that most authors don't make much money from their book sales. But authors can make substantial money using a book as a foundation for establishing authority in a field and then work to build an audience. With those key elements in place, sponsorship opportunities can bring great rewards.

Following are ways that corporate sponsors *want* to work with authors:

Paid Blogging – If you have established yourself as a skilled blogger, you can get paid by corporations to write blog posts on their sites or, if you have a high-traffic website, you can get paid to write blog posts on your own website that are sponsored by a large company. You might also be surprised to learn that the blog posts aren't usually even about the sponsoring company. The sponsoring company will simply request that you write interesting content that their target audience cares about, and they will benefit from visibility as the sponsor. As a writer, this is one of my favorite arrangements.

Professional Speaking – Every author who wants to build an audience can benefit from developing skills as a professional speaker. Speaking allows you to reach your target audience in a more personal way, and keynote speakers typically earn $5,000 to $10,000 and up for a one-hour engagement, plus travel expenses. Companies can hire you to speak to their employees or at an event or seminar. One of my author friends has an ongoing contract with a major company where they sponsor free events across the country to attract new customers. He comes in as the keynote speaker for an hour, dazzles the audience, and collects his check. The sponsor benefits by hosting the event and attracting new business. It's a win-win situation and a dream gig for an author who likes to speak.

Webinars – The popularity of webinars has continued to increase in recent years, and these events provide an efficient way for hosts to reach a global audience. You can sell your services as a webinar speaker to help a company reach its target audience.

Bulk Sales – There are many ways to sell your books in bulk to large companies. They can give away books to employees, distribute them as bonus items at trade shows, offer them as a bonus with purchase, or simply give them away to attract more clients. For example, if you authored a book on how to manage business finances, you could approach a large bank and inquire about them giving books away to their business banking clients. The key is finding the right company with needs that match what your book has to offer.

Product Licensing – Similar to how companies want to distribute books to employees and at events, they also need content to give away as a reward for new social media followers, newsletter sign-ups, contests, and other online campaigns. Consider licensing your ebook or a similar information product such as a workbook, special report, or video series. You can also offer customization, such as a chapter about the company within your ebook, and then license a specific number of copies that the company can distribute in any way they like.

Spokesperson – One of the more lucrative opportunities available to authors is the role of spokesperson, which is similar to how celebrities are hired to represent perfume or shampoo. In this role, you act as the celebrity and you may conduct media interviews on the company's behalf or attend company-sponsored events. These roles are typically hired on a retainer basis with five- to six-figure contracts, depending on the scope of the agreement.

Advisory Board – Companies that want to better reach their target audience often seek out experts who understand their audience and look for advice. This is a hybrid consulting role where you may help company leaders brainstorm ideas or choose directions for product development, marketing, publicity, social media, and other business issues.

Advertising – If you have a high traffic website or access to a large audience, you can absolutely get companies to pay you for exposure to your audience. Advertising can come in all kinds of forms: banner or text ads on your website, a page within your next book, an ad within your newsletter, or even a co-produced direct mail campaign. You have a lot of room to get creative here since most big companies have hefty advertising budgets to spend each year and they are looking for new ways to invest those dollars.

Event Sponsorship – If you conduct your own events, from workshops and conferences to online events, you can sell sponsorships to companies. These agreements can include logo placement, mentioning the company in your media releases and promotional materials, prominent displays at your event, and even sponsored merchandise. I recently attended the Small Business Influencer Awards event in New York where Blackberry was a top sponsor. The company name was printed on the beautiful trophies we received, and they also distributed travel bags with battery packs for charging electronics on the go. Not only did that investment get Blackberry exposure with the thousands of attendees, but it's now getting them additional exposure here!

Sponsored Tweets – Social media is a high priority for most large companies, and it's another place for them to invest their marketing dollars by paying influential industry leaders to share their content or talk about their products and services. In fact, in conjunction with most of the above corporate sponsorships these days, you will also be asked to share news with your social networks. Once you've built a substantial social media audience, you can offer to help promote the event where you are the speaker or the blog post you write for a corporate sponsor. This brings a lot of added value to your relationship. Companies also pay to host Twitter chats, events on Twitter where you set an hour aside to ask questions and communicate with your audience. Yes, you can absolutely monetize your social media presence.

What Corporate Sponsors Want from Authors

While you may think that these corporate sponsorships are few and far between, I can assure you that they are easier to get than you might think. Corporations aren't looking for a bargain. First, you should know that big companies have equally big budgets. On average they allocate 10% to 15% of profits toward marketing alone. That adds up to big advertising budgets, investments in new marketing campaigns, and an ongoing commitment to finding fresh strategies to implement.

They aren't necessarily looking for top celebrities, either. Here's what they really want:

Ideas – Big companies are run by people—and those people have to come up with all the big ideas. In many cases, they look to outside sources for new opportunities and solutions. If you want to pitch a company, give them an idea that aligns with their business goals. Read their most recent annual report to learn about where their growth areas are, what areas of the company are struggling, and what their priority initiatives are. Then put together a dazzling pitch that addresses a challenge they are facing (like how to reach a certain segment of the market) and how your offering can help them overcome that obstacle. Before you know it, that idea can work its way through the corporate approval process and a check will be on its way to you!

Audience – One way to assure you get the attention of a company is to demonstrate that you have a large audience. That could be a high traffic website, large social media following, thousands of books sold, an active speaking engagement schedule, or a large newsletter subscriber base. The fact is that having an audience gives you leverage. Figure out which companies want to reach your audience and then find solutions to offer them. And by the way, there's a good chance companies will seek you out when you start building some credibility in your field and show that you have an audience.

Professionalism – If you're going to pitch something to a corporation, it will likely go through several levels of approval. So whatever you offer has to demonstrate professionalism on every level. If you self-published your book, they won't care—as long as it has an attractive cover and has been through comprehensive editing. If you sell yourself as a speaker, make sure you are polished and deliver a great experience. The point is that you need to step up your game and demonstrate that you are the right person for the job.

How to Reach the Right People

Reaching corporate contacts can be tricky, but it has gotten easier in recent years. First, you should always start by figuring out who you know. If you can find someone to refer you directly to the contact you want to meet, that can be a great way to go. But since that isn't always likely, you still have options.

The best tool out there for finding corporate contacts is LinkedIn. Using the advanced search feature, you can search by company name, job title, or keyword. If you strike out on LinkedIn, look to Google to find leads. Some companies post an employee directory online. You can also call the company operator and ask for the name of the person in charge of XYZ department. And you can leverage other social media networks as well to find the information you need.

If your initial contact doesn't get noticed, get more creative. Mail a copy of your book along with a hand-written note. Send flowers or a fruit basket. Send tweets to the CEO. Do whatever you have to do to get their attention and ask that they at least listen to your pitch. Trust me, they are used to listening to pitches and ideas. If you want to cinch the deal, do your homework and show up fully prepared to pitch them something they can't refuse.

Author Interview

Name: Andrew Rogerson

Website: www.RogersonBusinessServices.com

Books:

- *Successfully Buy Your Business*
- *Successfully Buy Your Franchise*

- *Successfully Start Your Business*
- *Successfully Sell Your Business*

Are you traditionally published or self-published, and why did you make that choice?

Initially I started as self-published as I did not understand what was involved in writing, publishing, distributing and marketing a book. I kept hearing that the authors did not make money. However, I was then approached by a publisher who liked what I'd put together and agreed to publish and market the books for me. After time I went back to self-publishing as the publisher's margin was so high and it didn't make any sense to me to spend the time and money to grow the sales of the book and get back so little.

Tell us a bit about your most recent book:

There are four books that are part of the same series. The books are written for someone who wants to become an entrepreneur and build the American Dream of business ownership as they have three choices. They can start a business from scratch, buy an existing business or buy the rights to a franchise. Each book explores the specific option so a new entrepreneur can decide what's best for them.

The final book explains to current business owners, what steps to follow to sell their business. I am a certified business broker, so my books compliment my business.

Who is your target audience of readers?

My target audience is a new business owner who wants to understand their options of business ownership or those entrepreneurs that now decide they want to sell and move to the next phase of their life.

What has been the single most effective marketing strategy you have used for promoting your book?

My website is the most effective marketing strategy as the search engines are looking for content. If you have written books and are able to have the website organized with relevant key words, write blogs around your book topics, and create a media page on your website to attract speaking events, it all comes together to support the books and who you are as a business person.

What are some other marketing tactics that have or haven't worked for you?

There is no question that marketing is challenging. At its simplest level it takes time. At a deeper level it takes spending scarce money to test marketing ideas and to see what works. I was just recently offered my own radio talk show for one hour each week. The reason I received the offer was because the radio station found my website through doing a simple search. By having my website with the right SEO, the books and blogs for creditability and original content plus good graphics and presentation means the daily visitors to my site grows stronger each day.

How has social media impacted your success? Which social media networks do you feel generate the best results for you?

Social media is challenging because of the amount of time it takes and that it's very hard to measure. Because it is perceived as being free, it's tempting to put a lot of effort into it but my perception is that social media is still evolving and it's one tool of many to use.

What have been some of the biggest benefits of publishing a book?

There are many benefits to writing and publishing a book. The least talked about is that it forces you to research your subject matter and know your area of expertise. If you do not deliver on your content it's easy not to be taken seriously so this risk forces you to do the work. Very few people choose to invest the time to write a book. Those that publish a book stand out and have a competitive advantage. Other benefits of publishing a book are bringing a package of marketing together, the books, website, blog, video, social media and more all complement each other and collectively present a compelling package that "this person knows what they are talking about."

What advice would you offer to new authors who are getting ready to promote their books?

My advice to new authors is to only write and publish a book if you are prepared to do it for the long haul. It's a lot of work and generally a much slower process than expected. The financial rewards from book sales will be very limited in the early stages. The value of publishing a book is bringing it together with other marketing strategies and being willing to do the work and learning necessary to eventually be successful.

If you were starting over today, is there anything you would do differently?

What an interesting question and so hard to answer. If I knew what I knew at different times in the journey I probably would never have started. However, to build all the elements of the books, website, blogs, videos, social media and more and just have it available for anyone to find and then have it zig or zag in a direction you never planned is incredibly fun and rewarding.

Is there anything else you would like to add?

The return on investment of time and money to write a book and have it published may be limited. I think the critical thing is to do the research and write as best you can, then present your book and yourself as best you can to your market and then embrace and be glad for what you have done. Now continue to market and promote what you have put together but realize in the end it will be the market that decides your genius. Be content that the market does not always get it right; but that is not unusual for a market.

Resources

Google

Google's Free Keyword Tool: https://adwords.google.com/o/KeywordTool

Google Alerts: http://alerts.google.com

Analytics: http://analytics.google.com

Hire Help

Authors Assistants: http://authorsassistants.com/

International Virtual Assistants Association: http://ivaa.org/

Fiverr: http://fiverr.com

Odesk: http://odesk.com

Elance: http://elance.com

Trade Associations and Conferences

Independent Book Publishers Association: http://ibpa-online.org

Nonfiction Authors Association: http://nonfictionauthorsassociation.com

The Nonfiction Authors Network on LinkedIn: http://www.linkedin.com/groups/Nonfiction-Authors-Network-2950959

Nonfiction Authors Association: http://NonfictionWritersConference.com

Shaw Guides (list of writer's conferences): http://writing.shawguides.com/

Printing Marketing Materials

Vistaprint: http://vistaprint.com

iPrint: http://iprint.com

Next Day Flyers: http://nextdayflyers.com

Affordable Buttons: http://affordablebuttons.com.

Blog Directories (Submit Your Site)

Blog Catalog: http://blogcatalog.com

My Blog Log: http://mybloglog.com

Blogflux: http://blogflux.com

Technorati: http://technorati.com

Blogarama: http://blogarama.com

Blog Explosion: http://blogexplosion.com

Blog Hub: http://bloghub.com

Globe of Blogs: http://globeofblogs.com

Networked Blogs: http://networkedblogs.com

Blog Hop: http://bloghop.com

PR Resources

Help a Reporter: http://helpareporter.com

Cision's Media Database (formerly Bacon's): http://us.cision.com/index.asp

Gebbie Press (media databases):http://gebbiepress.com

Muck Rack (find media sources on Twitter): http://muckrack.com

ProfNet (subscription-based media directory for authorities): http://profnet.com

Newspaper Directories: www.newspapers.com, http://newsdirectory.com

Publicity Hound (PR tips): http://PublicityHound.com

Internet Radio

Blog Talk Radio: http://blogtalkradio.com

All Talk Radio: http://alltalkradio.net

WS Radio: http://wsradio.com

Womens Radio: http://womensradio.com

Lists of Internet Radio Shows: http://authoritypublishing.com/store/internet-radio-shows-and-podcasts-lists/

Amazon

Author Central: http://authorcentral.amazon.com/

Seller Central: http://sellercentral.amazon.com/

Kindle Direct Publishing: http://kdp.amazon.com

Book Awards

Ben Franklin Book Awards: http://ibpabenjaminfranklinawards.com/

Global Ebook Awards: http://globalebookawards.com/

Foreword Book of the Year: https://www.forewordreviews.com/services/book-awards/botya/

Nautilus Book Awards: http://www.nautilusbookawards.com/

National Indie Excellence Book Awards: http://www.indieexcellence.com/

The Eric Hoffer Awards: http://www.hofferaward.com/

Small Business Book Awards: http://bookawards.smallbiztrends.com/

Web Tools

Constant Contact (email marketing): http://constantcontact.com

United States Postal Service: http://usps.com

Stamps.com (print your own postage): http://stamps.com

Ecommerce Shopping Carts: http://ejunkie.com, http://oneshoppingcart.com, http://payloadz.com

Clickbank (affiliate sales for information products): http://clickbank.com

Social Media Tools

Tweetscan (search for tweets by keyword): http://tweetscan.com

Twit Pic (share photos on Twitter): http://twitpic.com

Twit Vid (share videos on Twitter): http://twitvid.com

SocialOomph (schedule social media posts): http://socialoomph.com

Poll Your Followers (social media surveys): http://pollyourfollowers.com

Tweetdeck (essential tool for monitoring Twitter): http://tweetdeck.com

Pay with a Tweet: http://paywithatweet.com

Tweetgrid (tool for managing Twitter chat events): http://tweetgrid.com

Social Media User Directories: http://wefollow.com, http://twiends.com, http://twellow.com, http://justtweetit.com, http://tweetfind.com

Facebook Page Migration (convert personal profile to business page): https://www.facebook.com/pages/create.php?migrate

Google+ Business Pages: https://plus.google.com/pages/create

Google Authorship: https://plus.google.com/authorship

YouTube Video Editor: http://www.youtube.com/editor

Vimeo (video hosting site): http://vimeo.com

Traffic Geyser (video marketing service): http://trafficgeyser.com

Social Media Contest Apps: http://www.binkd.com/free-twitter-contest-app/, http://interactwive.com/, http://corp.wishpond.com/photo-contest/, http://woobox.com/photocontests, http://pages.launchpad6.com/, http://www.strutta.com, http://corp.wishpond.com/vote-contest/

Facebook Contest Guidelines: https://www.facebook.com/page_guidelines.php

Sponsored Tweets: http://SponsoredTweets.com

Advertising

Google Adsense: www.google.com/adwords

Bing: http://bingads.microsoft.com/

Yahoo: http://advertising.yahoo.com/

AOL: http://advertising.aol.com/

Twitter: https://business.twitter.com/advertise/start/, http://ads.twitter.com

LinkedIn: www.linkedin.com/advertising

Facebook: https://www.facebook.com/advertising

Professional Speaking

Prezi (presentation software alternative to PowerPoint): http://prezi.com

National Speakers Association (NSA): http://www.nsaspeaker.org/

Toastmasters: www.Toastmasters.org

American Society for Training and Development: http://www.astd.org/

American Seminar Leaders Association: http://www.asla.com/

Speaker Net News (newsletter): http://SpeakerNetNews.com

Slideshare: (http://www.slideshare.net/

Submit Guest Blog Posts and Articles

Business Info Guide: http://businessinfoguide.com/directory/contribute/

Blog Carnival: http://blogcarnival.com

Ezine Articles: http://ezinearticles.com

Event Recording and Production

Instant Teleseminar: http://instantteleseminar.com

Free Conference Call: http://freeconferencecall.com

Skype Recording Services: http://voipcallrecording.com/, http://www.pamela.biz/en/, http://www.easyvoiprecorder.org/

Podcast Editing: http://audacity.com, http://www.apple.com/ilife/garageband/.

Liberated Syndication (for podcasts): http://libsyn.com/

iTunes (submit podcasts): http://www.apple.com/itunes/podcasts/specs.html

Go To Meeting (for webinars): http://gotomeeting.com

Instant Teleseminar (for teleseminars and webinars): http://instantteleseminar.com

Free Conference (for teleseminars): http://freeconference.com

Eventbrite (online event sales and management tool): http://eventbrite.com

Handy Tools and Miscellaneous Resources

Smashwords (ebook distribution): http://Smashwords.com

Book Baby (ebook distribution): http://bookbaby.com

Goodreads: http://goodreads.com

Red Room: http://redroom.com

Quora: http://quora.com

AllExperts: http://allexperts.com

Get your photo posted alongside blog comments: https://en.gravatar.com/

Survey Monkey (conduct online surveys): http://surveymonkey.com

Writers Market (directory of editorial contacts for freelancers): http://writersmarket.com

The meanings and interpretations of various colors: http://crystal-cure.com/color-meanings.html

About the Author

STEPHANIE CHANDLER IS THE author of the following books:

- *Own Your Niche: Hype-Free Internet Marketing Tactics to Establish Authority in Your Field and Promote Your Service-Based Business*

- *Booked Up! How to Write, Publish and Promote a Book to Grow Your Business*

- *LEAP! 101 Ways to Grow Your Business*

- *The Conference Catcher: An Organized Journal for Capturing Ideas, Resources, and Action Items at Educational Conferences, Trade Shows, and Events*

- *From Entrepreneur to Infopreneur: Make Money with Books, eBooks and Information Products*

- *The Author's Guide to Building an Online Platform: Leveraging the Internet to Sell More Books*

- *The Business Startup Checklist and Planning Guide: Seize Your Entrepreneurial Dreams!*

Stephanie is also CEO of Authority Publishing, specializing in custom publishing for nonfiction books and social media marketing services for authors, and BusinessInfoGuide.com, a directory of resources for entrepreneurs. In 2010, she launched the Nonfiction Writers Conference, a virtual event conducted with fifteen speakers over three days. She is also founder of the Nonfiction Authors Association, a community dedicated to marketing education and support for new and established authors. A frequent speaker at business events and on the radio, Stephanie has been featured in *Entrepreneur Magazine, BusinessWeek, Inc.com,* and *Wired* magazine, and she is a blogger for *Forbes.*

An advocate for animal rescue (please, go adopt from a shelter or rescue organization!), Stephanie resides near Sacramento, California and her favorite way to spend any day is with her school-aged son. She has three rescue cats, and a mutt named Mojo who was almost put down at a shelter for being too aggressive. Mojo is now twelve years old and a friendly and loving companion. Life is good!

Websites and Author Resources:

- **http://NonfictionAuthorsAssociation.com** – Association for Nonfiction Authors, providing a supportive community for members to connect, learn, and support each other.

- **http://NonfictionWritersConference.com** – The only online conference of its kind for nonfiction authors. Conducted annually with 15 speakers over three days.

- **http://AuthorityPublishing.com** – Specializing in custom publishing for nonfiction books and social media marketing services for authors.

- **http://BusinessInfoGuide.com** – Resources for entrepreneurs. Guest articles and interviews welcome. Look for the "contribute" link on the main navigation menu.

- **http://StephanieChandler.com** – Official author/speaker website.

Social Media:

- Twitter: http://twitter.com/bizauthor
- Facebook: http://www.facebook.com/AuthorStephanieChandler
- LinkedIn: http://www.linkedin.com/in/stephaniechandler
- Google+: https://plus.google.com/u/0/104611024263604411179
- Pinterest: http://pinterest.com/bizauthor/

Join the Nonfiction Authors Association!

The Nonfiction Authors Association is a community for authors to connect, learn, and exchange ideas. Our primary mission is to help members by providing educational resources and community support for marketing nonfiction books. Book publishing and marketing can be a lonely journey. We aim to make that journey a bit easier by connecting members with industry experts and fellow authors in a supportive environment.

There are two membership options: Basic (free) and Authority ($19/month). All members receive a free online profile, a member badge to feature on your website, and live access to our monthly teleseminars (two events per month featuring publishing industry experts and authors with success stories to share). Authority members receive event recordings, private forum access, marketing homework sent via email each week, and special member discounts.

Join us to discover the many ways that you can grow your audience and sell more books!

Register and claim your free profile at
www.NonfictionAuthorsAssociation.com

CPSIA information can be obtained
at www.ICGtesting.com
Printed in the USA
FSOW02n2142030916
24534FS